ALTERNATIVE DISPUTE RESOLUTION:
A PRACTICAL GUIDE

ALTERNATIVE DISPUTE RESOLUTION: A PRACTICAL GUIDE

Dr C Chatterjee

LL.M. (Cambridge), LL.M., Ph.D (London)

Barrister

and

A Lefcovitch

LL.M

Solicitor

Routledge
Taylor & Francis Group
LONDON AND NEW YORK

First published 2008

by **Routledge**

Albert House
1–4 Singer Street
London EC2A 4BQ
United Kingdom

Routledge is an imprint of the Taylor & Francis Group, an informa business

Typeset in Plantin and Optima by
AJS Solutions, Huddersfield – Dundee
Printed and bound in Great Britain by
MPG Books Ltd, Bodmin, Cornwall

Book ISBN 978-1-85743-370-8

CONTENTS

LIST OF CASES

INTRODUCTION

In view of the costs of court proceedings and arbitration proceedings, the need for operating a system of settling disputes, whereby costs will be reduced and the procedural formalities will have a secondary role to play, the system of adopting a procedure for settling disputes on a friendly basis which is less expensive and less time-consuming can hardly be over-emphasised. The ADR system may provide an opportunity whereby the deficiencies of court proceedings and arbitration proceedings may be avoided. Furthermore, it is the procedure that conveys settlement of disputes by an active participation of parties and the mediator's role would be that of a referee.

This work attempts to examine the merits and weaknesses of the ADR system in addition to discussing the requirements that should be satisfied in carrying out a proper ADR system for settling disputes. It also compares the merits and weaknesses of court proceedings and arbitral proceedings followed in settling disputes and the requirements it should satisfy in order to make an agreed settlement enforceable.

In support of the merits of the ADR system this work discusses generally the merits and weaknesses of the ADR system and explains the most popular types of ADR. One of the tenets that this work maintains is that the ADR based settlement can be enforceable. In developing this research references have been made to the primary sources of information and secondary sources of information have been referred to when necessary. This work is addressed to both students and practitioners who have an interest in the ADR system in settling disputes, be they of domestic or international nature.

A sociological approach to resolving differences, whether in a social group or a government or between two parties, must be regarded as an extra-legislative approach. The sociological approach to settling disputes is therefore based on an ad hoc approach. The primary purpose of settling a dispute or difference is to provide remedies to individuals and/or social groups and to acknowledge their rights. From this standpoint there is no need to adopt a totally legalistic or judicial method of settling disputes.

It should be pointed out that the term *"dispute"* must not be misused; for lawyers it has a definite meaning, that is, whether a dispute is a justiciable (legal) or non-justiciable (non-legal) dispute. It is elementary that a dispute may be a mixed dispute, that is, it may contain both legal and non-legal issues, but on balance, when a dispute contains a sufficient number of legal issues which merit a judicial consideration for providing remedies to a party, it is then usually regarded as a justiciable dispute.

Purely non-legal disputes should be regarded as *"differences"*, although many lawyers may find this distinction between *"disputes"* and *"differences"* rather controversial. Nevertheless, lawyers trained in public international law generally maintain this distinction.

Disputes usually arise for two reasons: (a) when parties ascribe two different interpretations to a contractual provision or a provision of a statute or a treaty, and (b) when differences become manifest as to the understanding of provisions and the assumptions on which provisions are based. Differences of understanding of provisions may be settled without taking a legalistic approach and this is where perhaps the alternative dispute resolution methods become most relevant; however, it may be unjust to settle disputes of a legal nature solely by non-legal methods.

It must be noted however that differences may lead to a dispute; therefore it will be advisable to settle the difference, where possible, by applying non-judicial methods, for instance, disputes of a matrimonial nature or industrial disputes may in most instances be settled by non-legal methods, and once parties have reached an agreement it may be legitimised by legal means so that a breach of the agreed settlement may be remedied by judicial means. In many cases, political disputes represent political differences in achieving political gains. Abundant examples are available to establish that boundary disputes, whether bilateral or multilateral, have been settled by conciliation committees or by arbitrators.

The establishment of the Advisory, Conciliation and Arbitration Service ("ACAS") in the United Kingdom signifies that not all so-called employment disputes require legal consideration; they are occasioned by different views maintained by employers and employees; however issues relating to rights of employee or employers are legal in nature, and should be settled by an application of law. When a so-called industrial dispute is referred to ACAS it really is not to be treated as a fully justiciable dispute. ACAS' services may be regarded as an alternative method of dispute resolution.

The term *"conflict"* seems to be over-used by many, be they lawyers or non-lawyers, although the term often appears in international relations: in the final analysis, a conflict is primarily a difference of opinion based on each party's perception of rights and claims. From this standpoint, all differences are, to a certain extent, based on the psychological perceptions of the parties. Sociological aspects of *"any difference"* are also based on differing perceptions of different social groups whose aspirations may have to be taken into account by a government in developing legislation, but commercial disputes may not necessarily make any room for such aspirations. Sociological elements of a dispute are in many cases philosophically orientated, perception-based and unlikely to offer any aid to resolving an actual dispute, particularly of a commercial nature. When dispute settlement is to be achieved by referring to legislative provisions, or provisions of a contract or a treaty, sociological aspirations of social groups are to be disregarded, but, of course, where provisions of law prove to be inadequate to deal with a particular situation requiring a determination of rights and remedies of a party, judicial institutions have, in certain cases, relied upon what is known as the teleological approach to law.

CHAPTER 1

The Growth and Development of Alternative Dispute Resolution (ADR)

1.1 INTRODUCTION

The growth and development of Alternative Dispute Resolution (ADR), in its rudimentary form, may be found in older forms of dispute settlement method, such as conciliation or arbitration in the market place. The current ADR system is a sophisticated and controlled version of the older system of dispute resolution between parties by private individuals, who were predominantly experts in the relevant field.

This chapter briefly traces the growth and development of ADR up to the current period and identifies among others, the primary elements of ADR, and the circumstances in which ADR may now be utilised as a dispute settlement mechanism.

1.2 THE GROWTH AND DEVELOPMENT OF ADR AS A METHOD OF SETTLING DISPUTES

If one accepts any non-court method of settling disputes as an alternative dispute resolution method, then ADR's origin may be found in mediation, conciliation and arbitration. Arbitration has a long history[1], but over the years this method of settling disputes has become as complex and expensive as court proceedings. In *Northern Regional Health Authority v Derek Crouch Construction Company Ltd*[2], Donaldson, MR, stated that:

> "... *arbitration is usually no more and no less than litigation in the private sector.*"

The complexity of judicial arbitration, coupled with its acceptance of the characteristics of court proceedings seem to have prompted the legal community to originate another alternative method of dispute settlement. Of course, during the 1970s and 1980s, in particular, consumer-led businesses and

---

[1] The origin of treaty-based arbitration may be found in the General Treaty of Friendship, Commerce and Navigation, 1794, between the United Kingdom and the United States; see further J Simpson and H Fox, *International Arbitration: Law and Practice*, London, Stevens & Sons (1959); the origins of arbitration generally may be traced as far as Greek antiquity.

[2] [1984] 1 QB 644 at 670

user-friendly concepts required to devise a less formal method of dispute settlement. In the United States, mediation, in the name of ADR, became an accepted and eventually a prominent method of dispute settlement in a relatively friendly environment, which did not entail the adversarial system with which courts are, in general, so concerned.

The alternative dispute resolution system (ADR system) stands for a system which offers an alternative to court proceedings. Strictly speaking, any non-court method of settling disputes will come under the ADR system of dispute settlement, namely, mediation, conciliation, negotiation, enquiry etc. From this standpoint, ADR does not represent any novel system of dispute settlement. Arbitration being expensive and time-consuming, the commercial world placed emphasis on the ADR system of settling disputes. Of course, it should be pointed out that in England, under the Civil Procedure Rules, initiated by the Woolf Report, court proceedings can in many cases be simple, less time-consuming and thus less costly than proceedings under arbitrations. In recent years, ADR as a conciliatory method of settling disputes, has been brought back to the limelight again.

Much has already been written on the historical growth and development of alternative dispute resolution, the origins of which can be traced as early as the third century BC and there is no point in going into details of the history of alternative dispute resolution. More purpose will be served by identifying and discussing the primary characteristics of alternative dispute resolution, the constituents of alternative dispute resolution and how the alternative dispute resolution may be applied in settling various types of disputes.

In considering the effectiveness or ineffectiveness of alternative dispute resolution one should consider the distinction between 'formal' justice and 'informal' justice. Justice cannot be formal or informal; justice is justice. It has been the perception of the advocates of alternative dispute resolution that justice can be formal or informal; in reality, what is sustainable is whether the machinery of justice is formal or informal. If justice has to be attained in respect of matters of legal rights, application of law cannot be avoided, only the environment can be changed. Alternative dispute resolution seems to be primarily concerned with how best an informal environment can be created for attaining justice but the rules of justice cannot be changed in the alternative dispute resolution process.

The fundamental issue therefore is whether in order to achieve justice, that is, protection of rights and offering of remedies, legal rules may be avoided. The alternative dispute resolution process aims at attaining justice in an informal environment.

If alternative dispute resolution is concerned with compromises, then it should not be concerned with formal justice as compromises are achieved by parties irrespective of what the law provides. Justice may not therefore be composed with compromises. Alternative dispute resolution claims to be informal, but informal about what?

Presumably, informality relates to the procedures. If disputes are to be settled on a friendly basis then that can be achieved with or without any reference to the law, but when law is to be applied alternative dispute resolution based settlements may not be called informal justice. They are in accordance with the law but attained in an informal environment, that is, outside the court environment.

It is important to consider whether alternative dispute resolution should not be concerned with the issues of protection of rights and offering of remedies. If alternative dispute resolution is concerned with this, then the procedures can equally be regarded as legal procedures. Consequently, all the perceived negative elements of legal procedure automatically come into the alternative dispute resolution process. Whenever legal rules are to be applied, their consequences must be accepted and in that situation it might be difficult to maintain a distinction between the alternative dispute resolution process of settling disputes and disputes settled by court proceedings.

Dispute resolution should lead to the protection of rights and remedies of the parties concerned. If alternative dispute resolution is employed for that purpose then there is no reason why it should not be regarded as a method which has adequate legal dimension. It must protect the rights and remedies of the parties by reference to relevant legislation. The caution must be entered that the process must not be misleading to the claimants and the defendants.

It is to be pointed out however that court proceedings, particularly in relation to matrimonial proceedings and protection of the interest of children, require the creation of an informal environment and therefore in a way they are very similar to alternative dispute resolution. Indeed, it becomes cost effective in that in respect of matrimonial and childcare proceedings every effort is made to curtail stages. The court welfare officers' function is that of an alternative dispute resolution expert and yet whatever decision may be rendered by the court, judicial recognition is accorded to the agreement of the parties and the issue of the lack of enforceability of that agreement does not arise.

It is crucially important to understand what alternative dispute resolution stands for. If its basic purpose is to protect the rights and remedies of parties concerned, this method of settling dispute cannot claim to be totally non-legalistic.

The debate about access to justice has a relatively long history but it seems to have attained particular prominence, particularly since the 1960s. Historically, justice has been state-sponsored and the subjects of a state have been required to accept the structure of justice and the system of justice without questioning the authority of the state. The linked[3] image of the king and the judge has dominated the world of judicial decision-making. Lawyers who act as instruments of justice generally assume a monopoly of dispute management, but in most countries the changes in the dispute management system have become

---

[3] See further, Michael Palmer & Simon Roberts, at pp 25–61

slow and lawyers experience two types of difficulty; the perception of the communities about *"justice"*, and the authority of the state-controlled judiciary and judicial system are often regarded as supreme. In most jurisdictions litigation seems to attain prominence over alternative systems of settling disputes.

Any movement towards greater access to justice must therefore be slow and alternatives must also be well-founded. It is to be re-emphasised that popular perception in most parts of the world favours settlement of disputes by litigation because of certainty of enforcement of judgements rather than settlement of disputes by any alternative methods.

Access to justice has something to do with human rights; by coincidence, the structured movement for the promotion of human rights issues started in the 1960s, although historically its origins date back to the seventeenth century and the civil rights movement in France and, more recently, to the United Nations formulation of the Universal Declaration of Human Rights in 1948. It was during the 1960s that the perception arose that access to justice may be regarded as a natural right whereby a state's authority in administering justice may be questioned. The age-old concept that justice must be done and shown is still true and without any access to justice the accountability of the judiciary may not be appropriately satisfied. Citizens' right to seek justice and remedies in a cost-effective manner cannot be denied by any democratic society. It is an integral part of human rights, including social rights[4].

There exists a dilemma between society's aspirations of seeking justice in an informal and less expensive way and a "deep pocket" concept associated with the legal profession. Access to justice must not be denied because of financial handicap. If access to justice is to be allowed then there is the need for comprehensive reform including reform of the purposes of legal studies and capping the fee structure of the legal profession, but it may then run counter to the *laissez-faire* doctrine. Access to justice cannot be conditional upon the financial capability of the seeker of justice. Dependence on public funds for seeking justice may no longer be viewed as the panacea to the problem. Law schools must be required to offer subjects related to welfare law[5] and the legal institution should find the ways of introducing legal studies without associating the profession with the *"deep pocket"* concept.

This issue is as important for the individual as it is for corporate bodies. The high legal cost that corporate bodies may bear in pursuing a litigation cannot be borne by the ordinary individual and, if nothing constructive is done in this regard, the individual may not be given any protection or remedies against illegal acts of corporate bodies or state ordinance.

---

[4] See further, M Cappalletti and B G Garth, *Access to Justice, Volume 1: A World Survey*, Sijthoff & Noordhoff, Milan, (1978), pp 6–9

[5] See further, D Bok, "A Flawed System of Law and Practice Training", (1983) 33, *Journal of Legal Education* 570, pp 582–583

The Woolf Committee Report in England is a step in the right direction, but it does not touch upon the future role of universities in preparing law students through their education and training. The disadvantaged must also be made aware of their rights, duties and remedies, and law schools and regulatory bodies for lawyers should also emphasise the importance of learning welfare law in greater depth.

1.3 ELEMENTS OF ADR

As the term suggests, this system of resolving disputes represents the alternatives to resolving disputes by court procedures, and the usual alternatives are conciliation, mediation, arbitration, med-arbitration and ombudsmen. Alternative Dispute Resolution thus may be considered to be part of the judicial system although in order to confer legitimacy on the negotiated or conciliated or mediated result a special procedure may be required to be adopted. It will be appropriate to discuss briefly each of these alternatives or elements of alternative dispute resolution briefly.

Arbitration is a procedure whereby the parties to a dispute agree to have their dispute settled by a chosen arbitrator or arbitrators who will be appointed either by the parties themselves or in the event of the parties failing to nominate their arbitrators, by the institution whose rules of procedures will govern the arbitration. Arbitrations are primarily of two types: legal and non-legal. Examples of legal arbitration are disputes that entail consideration of legal issues including the rights of parties, breach of contractual and non-contractual obligations and remedies thereof. Whereas non-legal arbitrations are concerned with fact-related issues and arbitrations on such matters are usually conducted by experts in the field of the branch of business concerned. Examples of the latter would be disputes settled under the procedures of GAFTA and Fat & Oil Seeds Federated Association (FOSFA).

Both conciliation and mediation have received attention in Chapter 2 of this work.

Med-arb is a dispute settlement procedure in which the elements of both mediation and arbitration are combined. In this procedure parties agree initially to mediate and, if that should fail, they would refer their dispute to arbitration.

In England and Wales there exist a number of Ombudsmen who hold independent offices and who investigate and rule on complaints from affected members of the public about procedural departures or mal-administration, whether in the public sector or in the private sector. Ombudsmen predominantly attempt to settle a dispute by pointing out to each party the strengths and weaknesses on each side, and tend to genuinely convince the parties how their dispute should be settled. If a party is not prepared to accept an ombudsman's finding, it can refer the matter to a court of law.

In addition to these institutions, there also exist trade association arbitration schemes in certain trade sectors just as there exist dispute settlement bodies for various professions: medical practitioners, lawyers, dentists, etc.

As stated earlier, irrespective of what form of dispute settlement is adopted, the common elements of all those forms is that the usual court procedures would not be followed and that disputes must be settled on an amicable basis by explaining the causes of differences between the parties and by identifying the strengths and weaknesses of each party's claims and defences. Arbitration concerned with legal issues often follows the procedure similar to litigation.

All forms of alternative dispute resolution rest on one common criterion, namely, the conciliator or the mediator as the expert must create a congenial and friendly environment must be prepared to listen to parties' cases patiently and must be able to clarify the issues to parties in a simple and accurate way. The disadvantages of going into litigation in relation to each case should be clearly highlighted to the parties to a dispute. All mediators, conciliators and experts involved in alternative dispute resolution process must first be effective negotiators.

The alternative dispute resolution system is based on the assumption that court proceedings are necessarily costly, time-consuming and oppressive. Furthermore, the obvious alternative method for settling disputes, namely, arbitration, became very close to litigation in its approach. Therefore, the system was promoted with a view to providing parties with a means of contesting their rights with some alternative methods of dispute resolution which would be less expensive, less time-consuming and non-oppressive. The elements of alternative dispute resolution have already been identified, and it may be maintained that although the alternative dispute resolution system seems to be a viable alternative to litigation or arbitration, the success of alternative dispute resolution system very much depends upon the quality and capacity of the actors in an alternative dispute process. Alternative dispute resolution is not based on any fundamental philosophy; its basic objective is to provide an alternative to the usual methods of settling disputes based on the assumption that this alternative may be more effective than court proceedings. To say that an alternative dispute resolution entails empowerment[6] of an individual seems to be a misnomer. It is not a question of empowering an individual, it is rather an issue of employing the expertise of an individual in settling the dispute but always by creating and maintaining a friendly environment.

Alternative dispute resolution (ADR) is primarily a method of "... *co-operating problem solving*", that is, each party to the alternative dispute resolution process must co-operate to reach a solution to the problem(s) and the primary function of the leader of alternative dispute resolution is to emphasise this element of the alternative dispute resolution to the parties. From this point

---

[6] A F Ackland, *A Sudden Break of Commons Sense: Managing Conflict through Mediation*, Hutchinson Business Books, London, 1990 at 27

of view, alternative dispute resolution may be regarded as a more difficult process than court proceedings in that the leader of the alternative dispute resolution process must not only have an understanding of the issues involved in the disputes but also a negotiating technique whereby a friendly environment throughout the process is maintained.

It is not entirely true that courtrooms are necessarily oppressive or coercive because courts for family-related cases including children's welfare, in particular, adopt a very amicable and friendly environment precisely for attaining settlement of disputes by conciliatory means. Many informal proceedings at courts, particularly small causes courts and settlement of disputes by arbitration for small claims can be friendly and informal. Many modern courts are mindful of the criticisms that are levelled at them and they try to improve their image. This is mentioned particularly because one should not be totally unaware of the improvements that the court environments are achieving.

It is natural that criminal courts and commercial courts dealing with extremely complex legal issues will be involved in long arguments during the proceedings but then such disputes are not suitable for reaching a solution by means of alternative dispute resolution methods unless, of course, the parties volunteer to accept this latter method.

It is also worth pointing out that there should not be any bland assumption that the alternative dispute resolution system is necessarily, by nature, friendlier and more informal than court proceedings. As stated earlier, the friendly environment very much depends on the negotiation capacity of the conciliator and how he manages cases. Indeed, the cost saving element of alternative dispute resolution is based on the assumption that a negotiation process may not start on the wrong footing.

Another precautionary measure that needs to be taken into consideration before employing alternative dispute resolution is whether a dispute can effectively be resolved by employing an alternative dispute resolution process. In other words, any blanket admission of cases to alternative dispute resolution process may be a cause of regret and waste of money and time. This is where a pre-alternative dispute resolution stage becomes important; one should not jump over it for the sake of activating an examination of the issues. Appointment of an appropriate conciliator with knowledge and expertise in the area of the dispute and the determination of fact that a dispute is fit for ADR are two very important prerequisites for determining whether the alternative dispute resolution process should be activated in settling a dispute.

Perhaps the best way of considering the effectiveness of alternative dispute resolution would be to regard it as complementary to litigation or other adjudicatory forms, that is, provision should be made whereby in appropriate cases the parties should try the alternative dispute resolution process, and if it should fail then the litigation or arbitral process still remains open. This is the reason why both ICC Rules of Arbitration and ICSID Rules of Arbitration, amongst other Rules, provide for conciliation preceding the stage of arbitration.

As stated earlier, the most important component elements of alternative dispute resolution, namely, negotiation and conciliation, have been with us for a long time. However, it was during the 1970s that the alternative dispute resolution movement resurfaced, perhaps because of the growth and development of arbitration as an alternative method of dispute resolution but also in terms of the manner in which arbitration relating to legal disputes became close to court proceedings. The non-commercial community initially, and thereafter the commercial community were interested in finding alternative resolution methods. The movement initially took an identifiable shape in the United States and later, in Australia and New Zealand, amongst other major countries. In so far as the United Kingdom is concerned, during the initial period not much support for alternative dispute resolution became manifest but from the 1980s a growing recognition has been accorded to this method of dispute settlement. In the United States alternative dispute resolution is more institutionalised than in any other country – there exists a National Institute of Dispute Resolution ("NIDR") and a Society of Professionals in Dispute Resolution ("SPDR") in addition to specialised groups, for example, the Academy Family Mediator; regulatory framework also exists in the United States. Similar developments took place in Australia and Canada. In the United Kingdom alternative dispute resolution was initially implemented in a significant manner in relation to family disputes. Currently, in the United Kingdom institutional growth has mainly arisen in respect of family and community matters; a National Family Mediation is an 'umbrella' institution and smaller family matters associations also exist, the memberships of which are open to solicitors, mental health professionals and other relevant professionals. The Solicitors Family Law Association encourages solicitors to take training for mediation as part of their legal practice[7].

The Centre for Effective Dispute Resolution ("CEDR") offers the full range of alternative dispute resolution procedures, predominantly in relation to commercial disputes. CEDR is co-sponsored by the Confederation of British Industries and many large commercial law firms. Only recently (1991) has alternative dispute resolution been recognised by both the Law Society and the General Council of the Bar[8].

It is to be pointed out, however, that the perception of alternative dispute resolution in the United States and that in the United Kingdom may not be identical although both jurisdictions seem to have accepted the importance of the alternative dispute resolution process. Whereas in the United States it seems to be more of an institutional mechanism, in the United Kingdom it is still regarded as a process which should not be made institutional but may be used where found appropriate. A society's understanding of alternative dispute

[7] *Alternative Dispute Resolution*. A Report Prepared by Henry Brown for the Courts and Legal Services Committee, *The Law Society*, Legal Practice Directorate, July 1991

[8] A Report of the Committee on Alternative Dispute Resolution, General Council of the Bar, October 1991

resolution is extremely important. If a society is pre-disposed to the effectiveness of court procedures then the acceptance of ADR will be slow, and this issue has received further attention in a separate chapter of this work.

1.4 LIMITS TO ADR

The nature of a dispute itself may act as a restraint on initiating the alternative dispute resolution process, that is, if a dispute is predominantly judicial in nature, it is usually resolved by an application of the appropriate legislation, and by relying on judicial decisions. Where a dispute relates to the interpretation of a term of a contract, a breach of which would necessarily entail allowing legal remedies and where a dispute relates to the interpretation of a statute or legislation, alternative dispute resolution should not be activated because it is a matter that must be resolved by judicial means.

Matters relating to people's fundamental rights should not be matters for any form of alternative dispute resolution as a state is the guardian of this right, and it is for the state to justify the loss of those rights or to reinstate them with remedies, where appropriate. By the same token, it may be submitted that the alternative dispute resolution process should not be involved in matters of constitutional rights of the individual or where injunctive relief in any form including security for costs is entailed. Where a matter is required to be settled by reference to mandatory rules, it may be difficult to justify the application of any method of alternative dispute resolution. Public policy, public morality and issues of the national interest must be outside the remit of alternative dispute resolution.

Where parties themselves would prefer to have judicial remedies, there is no reason why the alternative dispute resolution process of settling disputes should be activated. The alternative dispute resolution process, in all its forms, is consensual. Naturally, criminal matters are completely beyond the remit of the alternative dispute resolution process. The effectiveness of engaging alternative dispute resolution process should be considered seriously when more than one jurisdiction may be involved in a dispute and the dispute itself is governed by private law (conflict of laws) of the jurisdictions concerned.

There are certain special types of dispute, for instance, damage caused to the environment or by pollution, or intellectual property-related disputes, which may not be settled by alternative dispute resolution although instances of settlement of such disputes outside the court are not rare. This process of settling disputes has always been encouraged, in practice, by the English judicial system irrespective of whether or not an alternative dispute resolution system existed.

It is to be emphasised that the alternative dispute process in this context is applicable to domestic matters. Therefore it is subject to the private and public law of the jurisdiction concerned. Given the domestic nature and domestic parameters of alternative dispute resolution it is opportune to mention that conciliation as part of the alternative dispute resolution process is not very successful when the state is a party to the dispute[9]. The simple reason for this is that a state authority can always invoke the public interest argument and therefore the very basis for conciliation or negotiation becomes remote, if not totally unavailable. Indeed, conciliation as part of the settlement process has no part in administrative law nor can it be applied between public bodies as a pre-requisite for alternative dispute resolution in that both parties are public in character, although the prospect of initiating conciliation or any other elements of alternative dispute resolution may not be entirely dismissed when the other party is a public body. Furthermore, alternative dispute resolution may not be applied to issues which are to be primarily governed by the private international law of a country, such as issues of inheritance, or property rights in a conflictual situation. In theory, ADR may be applied to resolve disputes relating to these matters but in reality each party will try to gain as many legal remedies as possible between the two relevant legal systems.

1.5 CONCLUSIONS

ADR is a system which entails a variety of mechanisms, namely, conciliation, negotiation, mediation etc. The ADR system provides an alternative to the system of settling disputes by court proceedings. The limitations of the ADR system have already been identified. Activation of the system, at least in England, is based on the consent of the parties concerned. It is extremely important to ensure that the ADR system is not imposed on the parties to a dispute, as otherwise the prospect of enforcing the agreement reached by parties will become remote. The success or failure of the ADR system of dispute settlement very much depends on the issue of its conclusions being successfully enforced. This issue has received attention in Chapter 11 of this work.

From an academic standpoint it may be stated that arbitration should come under the ADR system, as it is an alternative method to court proceedings. It is appreciated that arbitration has already been recognised as a separate system of dispute settlement, but the fact remains that it provides an alternative method of dispute settlement to court proceedings. Parties' willingness to accept ADR-based decision as a binding decision is crucially important.

[9] See further Jean-Pierre Cot, *International Conciliation*, Europa Publications, London, 1972, at p 20

CHAPTER 2

Some Basic Concepts

2.1 INTRODUCTION

In recent years ADR received much attention from the international community in order to establish that this may be a viable alternative to court proceedings in settling disputes whether of a commercial nature or not. Historically speaking, this is not a novel phenomenon. The practice of settling disputes by methods other than court proceedings has been with the international community since the fifteenth century[1]. The institution of dispute resolution by informal means started at the market place where in the event of a dispute arising in relation to the quality and quantity of an expert's opinion used to be sought at the market place and his decision was regarded as final. The method of settling financial disputes between parties by mixed claims commissions dates as far back as the nineteenth century[2].

Historically, mediation has been used for settling political disputes including boundary disputes. In the mediation process the mediator's opinion is in a way imposed on the parties and the latter in recognition of the specialist knowledge of the mediator are expected to follow his recommendation. The traditional methods of settling commercial disputes have been conciliation, arbitration and judicial proceedings. However, the role of enquiry and good offices in settling disputes may not be disregarded, particularly in regard to non-commercial disputes.

It is interesting to note that in recent years, instead of placing emphasis on conciliation, mediation of disputes has received much attention, which seems to be rather puzzling. It is often found that where the term should actually be conciliation, mediation is referred to in its place. This point is important because the procedural differences between conciliation and mediation are significant. In a conciliation process, the conciliator is required to clarify the misunderstanding or differences in an attempt to allow the parties to reach a solution on an amicable basis. Mediation does not entail this process. It is nothing but a considered view of the issues rendered by a mediator in the hope that parties would accept them.

Incidentally, in view of the inherent qualities of conciliation both the Rules of the International Chamber of Commerce ("ICC") and the International Centre for Settlement of Investment Disputes ("ICSID"), for example,

---

[1] See further J-P Cot, *International Conciliation*, Europa Publications, London, (1972) at 36

[2] See further J. L. Simpson and H Fox, *International Arbitration*, Stevens, London, (1959) at 4

provide for conciliation as a stage prior to commencing arbitration. Neither of these institutions provide for mediation. However, before going into the other aspects of ADR, it is important to explain certain basic concepts relevant to the ADR system.

2.2 CERTAIN BASIC CONCEPTS

2.2.1 Alternative Dispute Resolution

ADR is a system of dispute resolution which is alternative to court proceedings. In England, ADR has received recognition as an alternative to court proceedings, but it has not yet been established whether this alternative is as effective as court proceedings; this is not to suggest that ADR will not be as effective as court proceedings, in due course. Furthermore, the issue of human perception that a judgment rendered under an acknowledged legal framework may be more acceptable than an agreed conclusion of a dispute under the ADR system still remains.

The ADR system has a direct advantage however in that while going through this process, the parties become aware of the strengths and weaknesses of their respective cases; thus it may operate as a pre-court proceedings stage; which may minimise the high incidence of court proceedings.

2.2.2 Negotiation, including intra-party and multi-party negotiations

In the context of settlement of legal disputes, the term *"negotiation"* often seems to be misused. Negotiation has a simple meaning; it stands for conferring with others in order to reach a compromise or agreement. It is not a method of settling disputes; it is a process which may be applied to iron out the differences between the parties; it is often applied to settling political differences.

At the early stages of conciliation or mediation, a degree of antagonism on each side may become evident, and therein comes the negotiation technique whereby the ultimate objectives of both parties must be clearly identified concisely and meaningfully. In this process, contrary to the popular belief, there is no room for bargaining[3]. It is through the negotiation process that the common objectives of both parties should be identified and thereafter the conciliation process concretises them. In other words, conciliation should be preceded by a negotiating process which will entail identification of strategies and weaknesses instead of maintaining any perception of superiority. Any notion of bargaining power or superiority that may be held by a party will defeat the purposes of negotiation and conciliation. Once the strengths and weaknesses of both parties have been clearly identified and put on the table, an effective conciliation process should take place.

---

[3] See further C Chatterjee, *Negotiating Techniques in International Contracts*, Ashgate, Aldershot, (2000) at 132–133

It is not the purpose of this work to evaluate the opinions of psychologists or sociologists as to the effectiveness of negotiation and what it entails; it must be emphasised however that in the hard business world those theoretical approaches have hardly any application. If bargaining power is emphasised in negotiation, no commercial contract may be concluded because in the contemporary business world, many buyers and sellers and service providers are available. This is why in the negotiating process one is required to identify what are the strengths and weaknesses for each party.

Returning to dispute resolution, it is to be emphasised that negotiation has some room to play, which has already been explained. It is a process that leads to conciliation. Conciliation from this standpoint formalises a dispute resolution by pointing out the areas of agreement which would be acceptable by parties; but at the heart of any dispute resolution is negotiation although it is not formally recognised as a method of settling disputes. This has received much more detailed attention at a later stage of this work.

In recent years, many practitioners have perceived arbitration on legal issues as an entirely different method of settling disputes from alternative dispute resolution methods, but strictly speaking arbitration may also come under alternative dispute resolution method.

Most of the components of alternative dispute resolution have a very long and impressive history; they have been applied in respect of settling both bilateral and multilateral disputes. It will therefore be appropriate to discuss dispute settlement by alternative dispute resolution methods at two levels: bilateral and multilateral.

It will also be interesting to trace the growth and development of those components of alternative dispute resolution to see whether they are still applicable in the contemporary commercial world. One of the most important components of alternative dispute resolution is conciliation which has attracted the attention of sociologists. The caution should be entered however that although the sociological aspects of conciliation may not be entirely dismissed, lawyers must pay attention to the legal effects of conciliation if they are determined to apply it as an alternative to settling a dispute by a totally legal method, such as court procedures. In other words, enforcement of a conciliated agreement is an important issue which must not be lost sight of.

Gulliver[4] maintains that negotiation entails exchange of information and opinion which might hopefully and eventually lead to an outcome acceptable to both parties. In this process each party tries to persuade the other in favour of his own case. According to Gulliver there should be an adjudicator conducting negotiations who will eventually pronounce his decision on that issue. He maintains a distinction between negotiation and adjudication but his distinction is based on the absence of a third party decision-maker in the case of a negotiation. He also draws a distinction between the two methods by

[4] P Gulliver, *Disputes and Negotiations: A Cross-Cultural Perspective* (1979), Academic Press, New York and London, at 3–7

maintaining that a decision-maker is typically a third party, and that party is conferred with the authority and responsibility for reaching a decision. What is not clear, however, is the function or distinction between an adjudicator and a negotiator; of course, a negotiator is not supposed to take the role of a lawyer which an adjudicator may have to take. In a negotiation process two parties negotiate, and the presence of a third party, who is an adjudicator, is not essential. Whereas negotiation does not entail any judicial decision-making, adjudication does. Therefore, it is safe to assume that the matters which are fit for an adjudication settlement need not be referred to negotiation. In a negotiation process parties negotiate their differences and reach a settlement amicably. In an adjudication process the adjudicator's special knowledge is relied upon by the parties. In the negotiation process parties negotiate face to face; in the adjudication process parties may be remote from the adjudicator. Therefore, negotiated settlement is direct and participatory; disputes settled by adjudicators are settled by the intervention of third parties and are non-participatory. Whereas negotiation may not be subject to any specific rules or regulations, adjudication is. Parties to a negotiation do not proceed from a position of authority, whereas an adjudicator holds a significant degree of authority. In an adjudication process parties are required to submit to the jurisdiction of the adjudicator, whereas discussion and elimination of the differences between the parties is the basic means of settling disputes by negotiation. In a negotiation process, the parties proceed from their respective point of interest, but an adjudicator does not have any personal interest; he is required to examine the interest and legal rights of parties and give his reasoned decision. The Housing Grants Construction and Regeneration Act, 1996 provides for adjudication, which is a part of the judicial system. Under this Act, an adjudicator's findings may be appealed against to a judicial authority. An adjudication process is less formal than any judicial process; hence it is more attractive than a full-fledged judicial process.

Whereas an adjudicator is usually chosen by virtue of his knowledge and experience in the area of law with which the dispute is concerned, negotiators need not be experts; they are mere parties to a difference which can be resolved by clarifying certain facts and information.

Whereas in the negotiation process the management of negotiation is a matter for the parties concerned; it is for an adjudicator to manage the adjudication process. Negotiations often fail because of the lack of strategies and perceived ideas held by a party as to its higher bargaining power; an adjudicator is not concerned with the position or status of parties; his authority to manage adjudication is derived from a mandate he receives from the parties, and where it is legislation-based it is also derived from the latter. Palmer and Roberts[5] consider the role of power in negotiation but it is maintained that if negotiation is power-based then there may not be any long-lasting negotiation.

[5] See further Michael Palmer and Simon Roberts, *ADR and the Primary Forms of Decision-Making* (Law in Context). Northwestern University Press, Evanston, 1998.

In fact, "bargaining power" stands for the power to negotiate which has very little to do with the status and position of a party. Where the rights of parties are law-based it is hard to justify that bargaining power representing the superiority of a party has anything to do with negotiation. A reference to bargaining power in negotiation in misconceived. A corporate body may be stronger than an individual but the latter's position is determined either by the contract or statute-based rights or by the general notion of fairness and equity. Fisher and Ury[6] rightly see negotiation as a problem solving effort. It therefore requires a co-operative approach in which the interests of each party must be protected. It is therefore necessary in a negotiation process to identify the common interest of the parties. In negotiations, there must be a willingness to resolve the differences between the parties which is to be based on projected mutual gains. The idea of winning and losing is not the cornerstone of an effective negotiation process. In a negotiation process competition is not to be promoted; its main function is to narrow down the areas of differences between the parties, and such a co-operative approach based on the understanding of gains and losses of both parties is essential.

Bilateral negotiations are more straightforward, less time-consuming and less complex than multi-party negotiations. But, as stated earlier, unless parties comprehend their strategies well enough, the efforts may not lead to any effective negotiations and settlement of differences. One may not maintain that in any one form of negotiation, whether intra-party or multi-party, homogeneity of ideas may be created and that the team will definitely reach its goal[7]. Participants of a negotiating team must have the intention to reach an amicable settlement rather than form further basis for disagreement which will widen the gap between them.

Multi-party disputes stand for international disputes of a political or a commercial nature. As stated earlier, the process of negotiation between two types of disputes remains the same, only the scale is different. In the case of a multi-party dispute the issues are more complex than those in intra-party disputes and, of course, attainment of consensus becomes complex and delayed in multi-party disputes. This is primarily because of the lack of understanding of the issues by the participators and also when each party rigidly adheres to its own interest. Compromise of interests is essential in all forms of negotiation.

Negotiation in respect of social issues such as education, management of schools or any public sector matter, becomes complex but such issues can also be resolved provided public authorities appreciate the causes of resentment in society and are willing to amend the policies. This is primarily done through action groups, and agenda building by action groups becomes important so that a united front can lobby Parliament or government authorities. This is a

---

[6] R Fisher and W Ury, *Getting to Yes*, Houghton Mifflin, Boston, Mass. (1981)

[7] E Goffman, *The Presentation of Self in Everyday Life*, Anchor Books, New York, (1959)

situation in which the issue of bargaining power is not important. Public authorities are to render appropriate services to the community; they are necessarily required to look into the aspirations of the society. This process of negotiation for societal purposes may be lengthy because of intervention by various interest groups but the interests of the majority must be respected[8].

2.2.3 Conciliation

It has been acknowledged by authors such as Palmer and Roberts that the term *"mediation"* has been inappropriately used to mean *"conciliation"*[9]. Other authors such as Bush[10], Simmel[11], Gulliver[12], Palmer[13] and Riskin[14] discussed the attributes and characteristics of *"mediation"* which are really the characteristics and attributes of *"conciliation"*. On the basis of their works it is possible to identify those attributes and characteristics of conciliation which have been described by them as mediation.

"Non-partisanship" is essential for conciliation, that is, a conciliator must be remote from the contrasting interests of the parties but must participate equally to protect the interests of the parties concerned. A conciliator must not intervene in questioning the interests of the parties; it is his duty to point out the reality of the interest and analyse whether and why the interests of two parties stand differently. He or she is required to be extremely familiar with the basic causes of the dispute and the interests of the parties. In resolving a dispute he or she must be primarily concerned with how best the interests of both parties may be protected and yet a dispute be amicably resolved. The meaning of the term "conciliation" is very significant in that a conciliator's function is to clarify the issues and the causes of misunderstanding between the parties. He or she is there as a third party to explain the position and it is essential that in order to achieve a successful conciliation, the conciliator must command the respect of the parties to a dispute.

A conciliator is not an arbitrator, nor is he a mediator. Whereas an arbitrator arbitrates legal issues, when necessary, from a legal standpoint, a mediator suggests what would be best in the circumstances of a dispute between the

---

8 T Colosi, "Negotiations in the Public and Private Sectors" (1983) 27(2), *American Behavioral Scientist* 229, pp 241–243

9 Michael Palmer and Simon Roberts

10 R A B Bush, "Efficiency and Protection, or Empowerment and Recognition?: The Mediator's Role and Ethical Standards in Mediation" (1989) 41 *Florida Law Review* 253, pp 266–270

11 G Simmel, *The Sociology of Georg Simmel*, edited by K Wolff (1950, originally 1908), Free Press, Glencoe, Illinois, p 151

12 P Gulliver, *Disputes and Negotiations: A Cross-Cultural Perspective* (1979), Academic Press, New York and London, pp 214–217, pp 200–225, p 227

13 M Palmer, "The Revival of Mediation in the People's Republic of China: Extra-Judicial Mediation" in W E Butler (ed) Yearbook on Socialist Legal Systems 1987 (1988), Transnational Books, New York, Dobbs Ferry, pp 244–252

14 L L Riskin, "Mediator Orientations, Strategies and Techniques" (1994) 12 (9), *Alternatives* 111, pp 111–113

parties. A conciliator, on the other hand, attempts to resolve a dispute by identifying the causes of differences between the parties and the legal position if the dispute was referred to a court of law or arbitration. A conciliator is thus a friend who does not intervene, but explains the position of the parties without any personal interest and in this process he or she is required to be realistic about the proposals of losing or winning their case, so as to gradually point out the consequences of not agreeing to settle that dispute on a friendly basis. It is essential for a conciliator to firmly establish and create a genuine impression on the parties' minds that he or she has no personal interest in the subject-matter of the dispute or the interests of the parties. A conciliator's findings should be regarded as a recommendation to the parties pointing out what other alternatives the parties may have if they do not accept a conciliator's finding. A conciliation process is very much like a peace-making process in which there must not exist any perception of power. It should be a thoroughly friendly participation by a third party settling a dispute amicably. There is no room for an intervention, of any nature, by a conciliator.

In a conciliation process the need for accommodation of ideas and concessions must be emphasised for mutual benefit. Quantification of losses both in financial terms and non-financial terms must be identified. There must be a voluntary appeal by a conciliator to the disputing parties for settling their differences, pointing out the coercive element that may arise in court proceedings if they should fail to consider the conciliated settlement.

A conciliator must be able to manage a conciliation process, that is, he/she must have control over the process; he/she must ensure that his/her participation does not antagonise the parties and if his/her participation does not seem to produce any effect, the process of conciliation should be halted; parties must be allowed a chance to reflect on their position. A conciliation process is directed like negotiation and the conciliator has the opportunity of studying the position of the parties even from facial expressions, body gestures or by other similar means. Where symptoms of rejection become manifest, the conciliator should reflect on his/her participation. In order to avoid such an unfortunate situation a conciliator should, at the initial stages, explain his/her position and objectives and try to create a congenial environment for conciliation by putting the parties' minds at rest. A conciliator must be able to develop confidence in the minds of the parties by explaining the nature of the issues involved in their dispute; concern must be shown by a conciliator if a dispute is not resolved in a conciliatory fashion.

The purpose of conciliation is not to change the nature of a dispute, that is, whether it is a legal or paralegal dispute, but to point out the strengths and weaknesses of the application of the conciliation process in settling a dispute or a difference. As stated earlier, a conciliation is primarily concerned with the settlement of a difference and that process may be necessary to identify the legal consequences, the nature of rights and remedies of parties if their differences are not settled outside the court. From this standpoint, a conciliator may be required to understand and appreciate the legal consequences if a dispute is not settled amicably. A conciliator's function is therefore to clarify to the parties their respective position and to convince them of the legal consequences if a dispute is not settled amicably. In other words, it is the function of a conciliator to alert the parties of the adverse consequences that might take place if a dispute is not settled outside the court.

2.2.4 Mediation

Mediation is a form of a third party intervention with the consent of the parties to a dispute. A mediator's function is to provide a solution to a dispute in the hope that the parties will accept it. He is supposed to be a neutral person with knowledge and expertise in the subject-matter of the dispute.

Mediation has a long history which can be traced back to the eighteenth century, if not earlier[15]. Historically, the institution of mediation was developed at a time when judicial systems in many parts of the world were in their rudimentary stage and decisions in regard to points of law were often based on justice and equity. In the mediation process the authority of the mediator is recognised. Parties submit to a mediator in the belief that the mediator's finding is rational and therefore there is no need to resort to any judicial decisions.

In a mediation process the relevance of the international expertise of the mediator becomes a crucial issue. It is a process which is not as participatory as a negotiation or conciliation process; it is a process in which parties do not directly negotiate, but rely on the finding of the mediator.

The circumstances in which a dispute should be referred to negotiation or conciliation or mediation should be considered very seriously. It is assumed that where negotiation has failed, the parties may refer their dispute to a mediator, although there does not exist any hierarchy between the two. The basic difference between negotiation and mediation is that whereas in the former process the parties settle their differences through active participation, the latter is more non-participatory and is reliant on a third party's intervention.

Of the two processes of settling disputes, perhaps negotiation is more effective than mediation in that in a negotiation process the parties, by consent, agree how to settle their disputes, whereas in a mediation process the parties' consent is not necessary. Take for example, the case of Camp David. Although the mediator was a renowned President of the United States of America and although the mediator's finding was initially accepted by the parties concerned, it may be maintained that it was not completely successful.

Settlement of disputes by negotiation seems to be more effective than settlement by a mediation process.

By the same token it must be pointed out that in a multi-party dispute all parties must attend and the technique of creating the environment and

[15] Simpson and Fox, *International Arbitration*, Sweet & Maxwell, London, (1959)

breaking the barriers remains as important for multi-party disputes as for bilateral disputes.

2.2.5 Multi-party Mediation

In a multi-party dispute settlement process, one may easily expect differences of opinions which are apparently unbridgeable, thus the whole negotiation process may end in a failure. But mediation may be compared with the collective bargaining system. Initially, there may not be any basis for agreement between the parties, but through discussions the parties realise their weaker points and eventually tend to come to an agreement. In a multi-party dispute settlement process, the mediator(s) must have a special type of expertise to manage the mediation process so that a situation of going round the circle does not arise, that the issues are clearly identified and that discussions are kept under control, that is, related to specific issues. Like bilateral disputes, multi-lateral disputes have two aspects: procedural and substantive. In a multi-party dispute settlement process mediators must be particularly mindful of applying the procedures and seeking confirmation as to whether any derogation has taken place. It is for the mediator(s) to ensure that the substantive issues receive adequate and appropriate attention and that the mediation process is kept confined to its limits. Mediator(s) engaged in a multi-party settlement process must have special skills, understanding of the problems and the capacity to manage cases and situations.

It is very important that the parties who are directly involved in a dispute are present at the dispute settlement process and that they have thorough knowledge of the nature of the dispute. Otherwise the whole effort will be wasted and time will be unnecessarily spent.

Controversy exists as to whether lawyers should attend mediations to represent the cases on behalf of their clients. Mediation is primarily a non-legal process for reaching a settlement. A lawyer's intervention is thus not essential, however if a dispute is primarily a legal one, then it might be advisable to hire lawyers to represent their respective clients. By the same token it is stated that experts' opinions should also be sought on technical issues particularly when a dispute relates to complex commercial issues or engineering or construction matters. In mediation, no vacuum should be allowed to be created by the absence of a party. A mediator therefore should point out to the absent party or "would be" absent party the need to attend a mediation.

Although a mediation process primarily consists of oral proceedings, like court proceedings, a mediation process is often required to rely on documentary evidence. From this standpoint, it is difficult to maintain a clear-cut distinction between mediation and court proceedings. The only significant difference between the two systems is that whereas mediation should be carried in an informal environment, court proceedings are usually carried out in a formal environment. But, like court proceedings, in a mediation process each party must prepare its respective arguments and submissions in order to allow the mediator(s) to reach a fair and equitable decision.

2.2.6 Distinction between Mediation and Conciliation

As mechanisms for settling disputes, mediation and conciliation have a long history. They are the oldest forms of mechanism for settling disputes, both national and international, even before the court proceedings system started. Mediation and conciliation existed in China some 3,000 years ago. It is important, however, to explain initially the circumstances in which mediation and conciliation were used as a mechanism for settling disputes. Mediation stands for a mechanism in which a chosen third party is allowed to intervene between the two parties to a dispute to render his considered view on the basis of which a dispute should be settled. A mediator's expertise in the subject-matter of a dispute becomes the primary basis for selecting him for the mediation.

Mediation was a common mechanism for settling disputes concerning demarcation of boundaries or political disputes. There is no guarantee, however, that the parties to a dispute would accept the considered views of the mediator.

The essence of conciliation on the other hand, is significantly different from that of mediation. Conciliation stands for clarifying misunderstandings that may exist between parties on certain issues, which in fact, have given rise to a dispute; in the conciliation process the conciliator is required to point out the areas of agreement and disagreement in the hope that the areas of disagreement between the parties will be narrowed down, in consequence of which the parties will be deterred from pursuing the matter in the form of court proceedings or arbitration proceedings. Unlike mediation, in the conciliation process no attempt is made by a conciliator to impose his ideas or decision on the parties to the dispute. He simply clarifies the causes of the differences between the parties and having realised the folly of proceeding with the legal action, parties then agree to settle the dispute amicably.

Whereas mediation is directed, conciliation is pro-active in that it allows the parties to realise that the differences between themselves are ones which are in doubt. One of the most important elements of conciliation is friendliness and the capacity of the conciliator to maintain a friendly environment in this process. Disagreement of parties on issues often becomes evident but it is for the conciliator to demonstrate his perseverance so that the friendly environment is never disturbed. In a conciliation process active participation of the parties becomes necessary and the conciliator must be prepared to pay attention to what the parties may say. In both conciliation and mediation processes third party intervention becomes inevitable, but whereas in the case of conciliation the third party attempts to clarify the causes of difference between the parties on contentious issues with the view to reaching an amicable settlement, in mediation third party intervention is predominantly to inform the party of the mediator's view of the contentious issue(s) and convince them to accept his views. From this standpoint, mediation is less interactive than conciliation. Both processes are facilitated but the methods in reaching a solution are different. In a conciliation procedure, the conciliator is required to be as neutral as possible; in mediation, although the neutrality of the mediator is important, his views are directly expressed to the participants.

A mediator is essentially regarded as a peace-maker; as stated earlier, mediation became popular in respect of disputes containing political differences between parties.

In recent years, however, the terms conciliation and mediation seem to have been used inter-changeably. This is quite confusing to lawyers trained in public international law; the distinction between conciliation and mediation must be kept clear. The term mediation is suddenly being used by the construction industry in both the United Kingdom and the United States[16]. The method of settling disputes out of court in the construction industry should be properly described as conciliation rather than mediation. Although this may sound like an academic argument there is no reason why the traditional meaning attached to settling of disputes should not be adhered to.

The alternative dispute resolution which has become popular in recent years also emphasises the role of mediation rather than conciliation. One should consider seriously whether a misuse of these terms might operate as a deterrent to many to using alternative dispute resolution by conciliation process. One of the primary objectives of the alternative dispute resolution system is to reach a business solution; conciliation is all about settling disputes from a pragmatic point of view whether a dispute relates to family matters or commercial matters, any other issue relating to the construction industry.

If the traditional meanings attached to conciliation and mediation are followed, then it is believed that conciliation as a method of settling disputes is preferable to mediation in that it has not only a business solution approach but is also interactive; the inherent process in conciliation being ironing out differences between the parties, so that the outcome becomes acceptable and enforced.

Conciliation as a method of settling disputes is often applied in reaching settlement in commercial disputes[17]. Conciliation is particularly useful in clarifying the differences between parties on particular issues, and as stated earlier, disputes arise primarily because of differences between the parties in respect of interpretation of the terms of a contract or of a statute or in regard to perception of matters. The connotation of the term *"conciliation"* necessarily implies that it is a method whereby differences between parties may be settled by friendly means.

---

[16] Stipanowich, T. at 66

[17] In this context the term "commercial" is used to include matrimonial and employment disputes.

The application of conciliation as a method of settling disputes has received attention in sections on matrimonial disputes and commercial arbitration.

2.2.7 Arbitration

Arbitration, as a method of settling disputes has a long history. It originally became popular at the market place; differences between parties as to the quality and quantity of goods used to be settled by means of experts on the basis of their knowledge and expertise in the trade concerned. This type of arbitration was not usually concerned with legal issues.

Arbitrations concerned with legal issues and court proceedings are very similar in terms of procedures; one of the reasons why arbitration is preferred by the business community is that in many countries the arbitration process seems to be rather faster than court proceedings; but this is not necessarily true in England. Of course, the party autonomy rule in arbitration provides another attraction for arbitration, but one may like to contemplate on the reality of the party autonomy rule, that is, the limitations of this rule. Where arbitration becomes a lengthy process, it may not prove to be a less expensive or less time-consuming affair than court proceedings.

It should be pointed out however that as arbitration proceedings, in general, prove to be as formal and procedural as court proceedings, ADR has in recent years been offered as an alternative, although strictly speaking, arbitration comes under ADR, as it is itself an alternative to court proceedings.

Although appointed by private parties themselves, arbitrators are treated as judges, and they are also allowed immunities from proceedings against them except on the grounds of misconduct, the international commercial community seems to have accepted the special position of arbitrators and arbitrations. This is particularly true of arbitrations conducted under the auspices of established arbitral institutions, namely, the International Chamber of Commerce (ICC); or the London Court of International Arbitration (LCIA); or UNCITRAL (UN Commission on International Trade Law); or when ad-hoc arbitral tribunals are constituted of reputable arbitrators. Arbitration can be extremely effective when courts in the jurisdiction in which arbitral tribunals operate have supervisory power over them (event though these arbitral tribunals may be constituted under the Rules of established arbitral institutions).

2.2.8 Amiable Composition

The origins of amiable composition may be found in civil law. In Latin America it is a very popular concept which stands for the method whereby the opinion of an expert in regard to the main issues of a dispute is sought. The primary purpose of it is to convince the parties to consider the opinions of the expert and try to avoid litigation. In England, amiable compositions are allowed in the litigation process[18]. Amiable composition is operated along with litigation and arbitration; UNCITRAL arbitration and the ICC Arbitration Rules provide for *amiable compositeur* too[19]. Article 33(2) of the UNCITRAL Arbitration Rules provides that:

> *"The arbitral tribunal shall decide as amiable compositeur or ex aequo et bono only if the parties have expressly authorised the arbitral tribunal to do so and if the law applicable to the arbitral procedure permits such arbitration."*

However amiable composition depends upon whether the parties to an arbitration have given their consent to the process.

Amiable composition is often used in conjunction with the power to decide *ex aequo et bono* which means fairness and good faith. This concept can be found even in Article 38(2) of the Statute of International Court of Justice. An amiable composition should not be legalistic although he or she must be conversant with the legal rules for which he or she has been appointed, but where legal rules are inadequate or inapplicable because of the novel circumstances an amiable composition may provide useful guidance, judicial or otherwise. An amiable composition may also rely on the principle of *ex aequo et bono* which represents equity[20].

Amiable composition with the provision for deciding the case *ex aequo et bono* is extremely relevant to the alternative dispute resolution process. In fact, if this practice is adopted many other disputes of a commercial nature can come under the international alternative dispute resolution process.

Under most legal systems parties to a dispute are required to confer power on an *amiable compositeur*, by an express agreement or, in the absence of any such formal power, the power to act must be inferred from the parties' submission. Amiable composition becomes most applicable when it becomes evident that a dispute may not be resolved on the basis of the applicable law alone and recourse to equity is necessary. It is in this kind of a situation that the arbitrator or a court should act on amiable composition. This is an important aspect of alternative dispute resolution too, particularly when it becomes evident that a dispute should be or can be settled without making it legalistic or by applying the substantive aspects of law governing a contract.

In England, an *amiable compositeur* is appointed for the purpose of seeking expert advice, whereas in Latin America an *amiable compositeur* is commonly appointed for the purpose of settling a dispute without the help of the rules of equity[21].

---

[18] *Trendtex Trading Corporation v Central Bank of Nigeria* [1977] 1 ALL ER 881

[19] Art 33(2) of the Arbitration Rules and Art 13(4) of the ICC Arbitration Rules

[20] See further H. Lauterpacht *The Development of International Law through the Judicial Organs of UN*, Stevens, London, (1958)

[21] See further Rubino-Sammartano, *International Arbitration Law*, Springer (1990) at 273

2.2.9 Informal Justice

It does not seem to be appropriate to use the term *"informal"* justice or *"formal"* justice as all decisions must produce justice and they must be formalised. It was, however, during the 1970s that debate about *"informal"* justice attained some prominence and some authors also formalised their opinion by publishing on the concept[22]. The origins of informal justice can be traced to China, where, in view of the societal culture, the question of formalising such justice did not arise. The view of the conciliator was to be taken seriously by the parties concerned and that is how settlement of disputes in many cases was reached. It is true that justice attained in that kind of environment is less formal than the environment in a typical courtroom. Attainment of justice in relation to small matters, in relation to large commercial issues or by bringing actions against authorities of state cannot be similar. The issue of enforcement with sanctions remains important in providing remedies to the aggrieved parties; therefore any reference to informal justice must be cautiously dealt with. Irrespective of the degree of informality in out-of-court settlement procedures, enforcement orientated societies will always seek formalised state-dictated enforcement procedures. This is where informal justice loses its strength to formal justice, although the importance of attaining justice in an informal environment and by informal means may not be over-emphasised. The parties must be allowed to feel that their rights have been vindicated. Justice attained by means of an informal system may not be able to totally dissociate itself from the state system, particularly when enforcement of the decision attained by such means proves to be important.

So-called informal justice is often synonymously used with community justice without appreciating that not all issues may be settled by means of the latter. The proponents of informal justice proceed on the assumption that, whereas the state is the realm of power and violence, civil society is the realm of freedom and equality[23], an assumption which may be difficult to sustain. This assumption suggests that everybody in the society follows the same principle of freedom and equality, which is not the case, although an ideal society must attempt to achieve that. Inequality in the society is very much a society-based perception because a state can only try to attain freedom and equality for all. The proponents of informal justice also proceed on the assumption that a state and its institutions are necessarily oppressive, coercive and not promoters of justice; again, that assumption may not necessarily be confirmed. The incidence of injustice may be created by both societies and the states including their organs. Informal environment may be a contributory factor to attaining

[22] For example, R L Abel, "The Contradictions of Informal Justice" and B de Sousa Santos, "Law and Community: The Changing Nature of State Power in Late Capitalism" in R L Abel (ed) *The Politics of Informal Justice, Volume 1: The American Experience*, Academic Press, New York, (1982) pp 270–271, 275 and pp 261–263; A W McThenia and T L Shaffer, "For Reconciliation" (1985) 94 *Yale Law Journal* 1660, pp 1662–1665

[23] B de Sousa Santos, op. cit.

justice, but exclusive informality may not necessarily give rise to justice. It is therefore important to consider whether the so-called informal justice is qualitatively as good as a formal justice which is conducted by courts and the state system. Abel maintains that informal justice has its own distinctive strengths and weaknesses[24]. According to him, informal justice purports *"to devolve state authority on non-state institutions"*[25] which includes delegation of power for social control but, in fact, it *"expands the grasp of the state at the expense of other sources of authority that appear to be potential competitors."*[26] The reality is that all private institutions must exist as institutions legitimised by the state; the limits to such institutions' activities are thus determined by the state itself. Take, for example, the informal institutions in England, namely, the various tribunals concerned with issues of land, VAT, rent, employment, immigration etc, are, in reality, funded by the Department of Constitutional Affairs and their regulatory body is the Department. It is therefore difficult for such institutions to be totally remote from and independent of state authorities.

If justice is done by private institutions, the fundamental legal question remains by what legal authority do such institutions deal with rights and remedies of people? Unless those private institutions are legitimised by the state, their legal authority and *locus standi* will always be questioned. On the other hand, if they are to be legitimised and if they have to be endowed with a proper *locus standi*, then a state must accord them that privilege.

Two issues therefore deserve consideration: (a) making state authorities less coercive, and (b) according total independence to institutions that may be set up or appointed for so-called informal justice.

There is no guarantee that the institutions concerned with so-called informal justice will not be bureaucratic or would not exceed their powers, and that they will not act as state institutions. From a psychological standpoint, a conciliator or the so-called informal justice maker, might regard himself as a judge and if there are no controls over his activities, then he will defeat the very objectives of the so-called objective justice. In order to regulate this conduct, state intervention is necessary, as in the final analysis, it is the state that remains responsible for doing and showing justice and protecting individuals living within its jurisdiction.

The proponents of so-called informal justice also seem to believe that state intervention is unnecessary in order to produce justice and that it is state intervention that takes away justice. The difficulty with this argument or notion is that a non-state institution is better than the state institutions. If one takes an example of a manufacturer of products, the whole problem of private enterprises will surface. There is no need to go into details of

---

[24] op. cit., pp 280–281

[25] op. cit., pp 275

[26] ibid.

"corporate social responsibility" in this context, but briefly, although private bodies are prompted by the *laissez-faire* doctrine, they invariably protect interests of their shareholders and they accord minimal priority to social responsibilities. In this context, social responsibility does not refer to matters such as consumer protection or negligence because the law in most countries has already been standardised to ensure that corporate bodies pay great attention to whether their acts might contribute to social ills. It is for this very reason that control of corporate bodies by state authorities is necessary; by the same token it may be stated that if justice is to be achieved by the total non-intervention of states, ultimately the people who are supposed to be beneficiaries of justice might suffer in the absence of any state control of the machinery of justice.

"Popular justice" is not only a vague concept but also a source of confusion. Justice has something to do with the legal rules; if justice is to conform to popular wishes, then there is no reason for referring to laws in producing popular justice. The distinction between the so-called *"informal justice"* and *"popular justice"* may often be blurred. However informal the mechanics of producing justice may be, the fact remains that the application of law cannot be avoided. Therefore, the institutions engaged in the so-called informal justice must render justice by referring to the law and regulations in respect of both procedural and substantive aspects. So-called informal justice seems to be based on the assumptions that a complex and prolonged procedure must be avoided in producing justice. Although an unnecessarily prolonged procedure is to be discouraged, the role of the procedure in the form of natural justice, hearing of the parties as witnesses, discovery of documents, for example, should not be avoided even in the process of so-called informal justice. Then there remains the issue of substantive justice which is based on legal rules developed by the state authority for the protection of the rights of the individual.

The proponents of so-called informal justice seem to be particularly concerned with the coercive nature of formal justice, but where justice is to be produced by the application of legal rules and procedures, a degree of coerciveness is bound to be encountered.

Informal justice may be particularly relevant to settling less complicated cases and small claims. It may also be suitable for those cases which do not allow participation of lawyers, for example, commodity arbitrations. It is to be borne in mind that decisions are based on facts rather than by an application of complex legal rules, and there is no reason why such a dispute may not be resolved outside the typical court environment.

The alternative dispute resolution is not necessarily applied exclusively to fact-based cases, its objectives and procedures are different from those of so-called informal justice. Conciliators or mediators can be legally qualified people. Alternative dispute resolution is not necessarily a process which should be interchangeably used with so-called informal justice; it is a process which may not entail any court environment but that does not mean that a conciliator or mediator would not be concerned with legal issues and/or legal rights and remedies of the parties concerned.

As a proponent of informal justice, Abel[27] tends to emphasise that informal institutions or actors of informal justice are different from coercive authority, and he identifies in his own way the causes of coerciveness demonstrated by state authorities and the causes of non-coerciveness demonstrated by informal institutions. But, as stated earlier, the so-called informal justice has its own limitations. Furthermore, if justice is not formalised, remedies may not be enforced either.

2.2.10 Settlement and Justice

According to Fiss[28] a *"settlement"* appears to achieve exactly the same purpose as a *"judgement"* but the question remains whether a *"settlement"* may achieve a permanent objective. Legitimisation of settlement by judicial means may sometimes be necessary, particularly when one of the parties is a corporate body. What is important is to identify the difference between the institution of settlement and the process of judgement. Although at the initial stage a private settlement may not entail any adjudication process, eventually it might. This is one of the limitations of the settlement system. Settlement is effective if it does not lead to adjudication. Settlement stands for the so-called informal justice; it is less expensive than litigation but a settlement may not dwell upon the legal rights and remedies of parties; its basic purpose is to reach a compromise between the parties. The term *"justice"*, therefore, is not to be associated with the term *"settlement"*. It is a resolution of the differences between the parties by means of compromise. Thus settlement is different from justice. If disputes are settled, justice may not necessarily be achieved as justice entails a consideration of rights and remedies of the parties concerned which rights and remedies are protected by the state.

In discussing the applicability of alternative dispute resolution it is important to maintain a distinction between justiciable and non-justiciable disputes. The so-called informal justice might be suitable for non-justiciable disputes, that is, a dispute which is not concerned with the legal rights and remedies of parties, and the so-called informal justice might be useful for reaching a settlement but not necessarily justice. The sociological approach to justice seems to be based on the assumption that institutional justice is coercive, time-consuming, expensive and formal. But, for the reasons stated above, if one wants to achieve justice it must necessarily be formal. The alternative dispute resolution process is also formal; it is different from the court procedure in that it is supposed to create an informal and friendly environment as it is intended

---

[27] See further R L Abel, "The Contradictions of Informal Justice" in R L Abel (ed) *The Politics of Informal Justice, Volume 1: The American Experience*, Academic Press, New York, (1982), pp 295–296, 297–298

[28] See further O M Fiss, "Against Settlement" (1984) 93 *Yale Law Journal* 1073, pp 1085–1086

to offer clarification to parties of their legal rights and remedies in relation to the legal issues involved in a dispute. Justice without the law is a fantasy, although differences might be resolved without lawyers. Alternative dispute resolution does not necessarily shun the requirements of justice; it simply tries to "informalise" the formal process of justice. Fiss has been criticised by McThenia and Shaffer who say that Fiss' model of dispute resolution is flat and unrealistic to the world[29]. According to McThenia and Shaffer the alternative dispute resolution movement primarily rests on the values of parties, the community and work place. Settlement, according to them, is neither an avoidance mechanism nor a truce. They look at it much as a process of reconciliation in which the anger of broken relationships may be confronted rather than avoided. There exists a fundamental difference between Fiss and McThenia and Shaffer as to the abuse of justice. Whereas Fiss comes close to equating justice with law, which often is impossible to achieve, McThenia and Shaffer do not believe that law and justice are synonymous. McThenia and Shaffer also believe that justice may not necessarily be derived from the government and that courts are not the only important places that dispense justice.

In operating an effective alternative dispute resolution process it is important to bear in mind the objectives that the alternative dispute resolution system may achieve, simple justice or justice according to law.

In tracing the historical growth and development of the mechanism of informal justice, Auerbach pointed out that because of turbulence in race and labour relations, the alternative dispute settlement in the United States was re-shaped, that is to say, the indigenous community initiatives survived or re-surfaced. Auerbach also pointed out that familiarity with cultural institutions proved to be one of the factors of clinging to such methods of disputes. However, during the second half of the nineteenth century the purpose of alternative dispute settlement was re-defined. For a long time and at least until the Civil War, the alternative dispute settlement was viewed as a means of community justice[30].

There is little need to go into any details of how alternative dispute resolution developed in the United States in particular relation to community issues but the fact remains that, in general, the sense of community justice was developed there in relation to matters of social interest. Thus, the intention to settle disputes of socioeconomic nature outside the courts was made evident. Again, the perception that the courts structure was against the interests of the working people proved to be a dominating factor for seeking alternative dispute settlement. The experience of application of informal justice systems

[29] See further A W McThenia and T L Shaffer, "For Reconciliation" (1985) 94 *Yale Law Journal* 1660, at pp 1662–1665

[30] J S Auerbach, *Justice Without Law? Resolving Disputes Without Lawyers*, Oxford University Press, Oxford, (1983), pp 57–59

in those areas seems to have developed jurisprudential inspiration in the eminent American jurists such as Roscoe Pound[31].

Like many other authors, Auerbach, also maintained that dissatisfaction with legal institutions increased during the early decades of the twentieth century; this was primarily because at the beginning of the age of industry various disputes of a technical nature arose and which deserved a conciliatory method of settlement. Any outside court settlement of disputes was regarded as a method rendering informal justice which people found satisfactory and less expensive but the fact remained that it required a significant amount of a sense of compromise on the part of parties concerned.

There remains a dilemma whether justice or acceptability of the compromise is the main purpose of alternative dispute resolution. Alternative dispute resolution is most effective when it renders justice by reference to the law and by referring to the rights and remedies of the parties under the law. Caution must be taken that the alternative dispute resolution system is not to be employed in order to exclusively attain a compromise because compromise may not vindicate the rights of parties.

2.3 CONCLUSIONS

The perception of an informal dispute settlement procedure still seems to be vague; but nevertheless it sufficiently attracts the attention of communities and societies. Any alternative dispute settlement mechanism must entail an effective procedure of enforcement of the agreement reached by the parties concerned. A further caution should also be entered that no ADR system should become coercive and stands for rough justice. ADR must also presume the fundamental and constitutional rights of parties. ADR is an alternative system to court procedure, but it cannot be alternative to justice. This chapter has made an attempt to explain the differences between informal justice and formal justice, and the conditions attached to each.

[31] Pound, Roscoe, (1906), "The Causes of Popular Dissatisfaction with the Administration of Justice", *American Bar Association Report*, Vol. 29, Part 1, pp 395–417

CHAPTER 3

ADR and the Court System

3.1 INTRODUCTION

The origins and the objectives of ADR have already been explained. It would now be interesting to examine the similarities and differences between the ADR system and court proceedings. Both systems have their inherent advantages and disadvantages. It is important that the reader considers the advantages and disadvantages of both the systems with an open mind.

It is the purpose of this chapter to familiarise the reader with the advantages and disadvantages of both systems of disputes settlement. It is to be noted however that the ADR system may also be operated by a court of law. This chapter also explains the various types of court-based ADR system

3.2 COURT-BASED ADR

ADR may be operated by courts or privately, but in both instances the dispute resolution process must be non-oppressive and friendly. Court-based alternative dispute resolution is governed by statutory or regulatory systems; consequently it may lack a sufficient degree of flexibility found in privately organised alternative dispute resolution. Whether an alternative dispute resolution is court-based or private it cannot be a mandatory system. It must be voluntary; the reason being that a mandatory alternative dispute resolution is a contradiction in terms; it is for the parties to choose court-based or private alternative dispute resolution. The controversy of mandatory alternative dispute resolution was considered by the Society of Professionals in Dispute Resolution ("SPDR") in the United States in 1990 in its draft report entitled *"Mandatory Participation and Settlement Coercion; Dispute Resolution as it Relates to the Courts."*

Cost effectiveness seems to be one of the best advantages of court-based mandatory alternative dispute resolution. On the other hand, court-based alternative dispute resolution may be bureaucratic. The report accepted the principle of mandatory alternative dispute resolution subject to certain safeguards but maintained that in no circumstances should parties be coerced to settle. In Texas, the US courts may order parties to undertake a non-binding alternative dispute resolution procedure, namely mediation, settlement conference, arbitration and even summary jury trials. As stated earlier, in the alternative dispute resolution process, the voluntary submission of parties is a crucially important factor. Any mandatory element in the alternative dispute resolution might import the rigidity and coerciveness of the court procedure. In Australia and the United States, a system of court-ordered arbitration operates whereby the relevant court orders for a case to be dealt with by way of arbitration, the finding of which initially remains non-binding. If no party takes steps for a re-hearing by a judge, the award becomes a binding court order; in the event of a re-hearing by a judge, where a decision does not offer a better benefit to the person who applied for a re-hearing, then sanctions may be imposed on that party. This process is known as court-annexed arbitration or court-ordered arbitration. This process started first in Pennsylvania in 1952. Parties may find it useful to accept a non-binding arbitral finding in order to avoid court-based sanctions, where permissible. In the United States deterrence exists in that if upon a re-hearing the party who referred the matter to a re-hearing does not improve his position, then costs will be awarded against him. Not all states in the United States have, however, acceptable this position (for example, Michigan) which is known as the fee-shifting position, but in Florida and Washington alternative dispute resolution statutes make provisions for fee-shifting[1]. Before referring the matter to re-hearing, perhaps, at the initial stage the aggrieved party should consider the pros and cons of a re-hearing of the matter.

In the United States, court-annexed hearings are informal, brief and summary in nature. The decision is instantaneous in most cases. Rules of evidence are not rigidly followed and parties are advised to exchange documents before arbitration takes place. Court-annexed arbitrations have attained popularity in many parts of the United States, particularly because of the informality of the procedures providing court hearings as an alternative[2]. In court-annexed arbitration the neutrality of the third party or the arbitrator is crucial and if that neutrality combined with fairness is demonstrated, the aggrieved party might not seek a court hearing. This point is emphasised because in the event of a court hearing taking place, the primary ethos of informal alternative dispute resolution is taken away although the right of the party to seek a court hearing remains. In other words, if justice is shown and done at the arbitration level, the incidence of court hearing might be fewer. Court ordered arbitrations are conciliatory and hence less regard is paid to strict procedures. This is another means of making formal justice informal.

3.3 COURT-ATTACHED MEDIATION

Historically, conciliation and mediation developed as two distinctly different institutions for settling disputes. To an international lawyer, they still remain

[1] See further Henry Brown and Arthur Marriott, "ADR Principles and Practice", Sweet & Maxwell, London (1993)

[2] Adler, Hensler & Nelson, "Simple Justice: How Litigants Fare in the Pittsburgh Court Arbitration Program" (1983) at pp 629–637 of Murray, Rau & Sherman, *Processes of Dispute Resolution: The Role of Lawyers* (1989)

separable and separate institutions. This issue has received attention in chapter 2 of this work. However, interestingly enough, in so far as alternative dispute resolution is concerned and the manner in which mediation is used as a component of alternative dispute resolution, no distinction is made between mediation and conciliation: a confusing position. In practice, in the United States in particular, where the process of settling disputes bears the traits of conciliation, it is described as mediation, and it is used as an adjunct to the court system. Mediation is thus in effect an element of the court system. From this point of view the term court-annexed mediation becomes relevant[3]. In England, conciliation rather than mediation has been in vogue for a considerable period of time, particularly in family proceedings including child-welfare proceedings. In the latter type of proceedings, participation of the court welfare officer is compulsory; attempts are made to ensure that a conciliatory environment is created, particularly when children are required to come to the court. In respect of straightforward matrimonial matters, particularly financial and property issues, conciliation is used. In relation to ancillary relief, settlement is often reached in the form of a pre-trial review in order to avoid litigation or to minimise the incidence of litigation. English courts prefer conciliation to mediation as a method of settling disputes because by following this method, the parties are made aware of the advantages and disadvantages of referring their disputes to courts[4]. Furthermore, it is inherent in English court proceedings to settle dispute out of court, where possible, although it is often done on the advice of the Counsels and/or solicitors engaged in litigation.

In England a sufficiently formalised alternative dispute resolution system is now in place, although it is somewhat different from the US practice. In the United States it has been a common practice to hold judicial settlement conferences in state and federal courts in almost all types of civil cases[5].

What is needed in England, perhaps, is the promotion of a system of conciliation formally in respect of all forms of litigation. The caution must be taken however that by virtue of creating another echelon in the hierarchy, neither the cost is increased nor the process of litigation prolonged. A court-annexed alternative dispute resolution system has become popular in Australia, where County Courts may order references to arbitrations with agreement of the parties or to refer proceedings to a special referee for inquiry and report. Court-annexed mediation procedure is also in vogue in certain states in Australia, such as Queensland, where a scheme for mediation in personal injury claims arising out of motor vehicle accidents is available.

[3] See further, G Kessler and L J Finelstein, "The Evolution of a Multi-door Courthouse", 37 *Cath. U.L. Rev.* 577 (1988)

[4] See further Gwynn Davis, "Mediation Appointments on Money and Property in the Bristol County Court", *Family Law*, April 1991 at p 130; see also District Judges Gerald Rose and Stephen Girlis, "Conciliation for Family Finance", *Family Law*, March 1991 at p 92

[5] See an article by Deborah R Hensler, "Court-Annexed ADR" in Wilkinson, *ADR Practice Book*, (1990) at pp 352–354

3.4 OTHER COURT-ATTACHED PROCESSES

Court-attached processes are popular in the United States; under these usually come neutral expert fact-finding, neutral evolution, private judging and the multi-door courthouse. There is no need to go into detail of each of those procedures; suffice to say that given the nature of the English system of settling disputes, whether inside or outside courts these types of out-of-court settlements might not be suitable for England in the current legal environment. The neutral expert fact-finding entails the appointment of an expert by the parties concerned to investigate and determine the factual issues. Although expert fact-findings are advisory in nature, in the United States Federal and State procedures provide for appointment of neutral experts who would give evidence before the court which may then be examined by the court[6]. In England, it is settled law, at present, that expert opinions are usually inadmissible evidence[7].

The neutral evidence system, which originated in the US, began in 1985 in the District Court for the Northern District of California. The purpose of this early neutral evidence, as it is known in the United States, is to ascertain the strengths and weaknesses of a case and to consider how best to conduct litigation promptly and economically. Almost all types of dispute are referred to this system, and there exists a time limit by which evidence must be submitted on the basis of the pleadings and statements obtained from the parties. At the evidence session, the parties themselves or their legal representatives, each make oral representations justifying their reasoning for the views in order to enable the evaluator to evaluate each party's case. This is very similar to what are known as submissions under the English court system. The early neutral evaluation is in many ways a "mini-version" of the court settlement procedure except for the fact that the court environment is not strictly maintained.

The evaluation session is privileged and therefore no official record of it is maintained. Usually, a 5-hour period is allocated to this stage. In so far as the United States is concerned, the early neutral evidence system is widely recognised as it creates opportunities for early settlement of disputes. In many cases, an evaluator works on a pro-bono basis but this may not be an issue in justifying or rejecting the usefulness of the system[8].

Incidentally, it has been the practice under the English legal system to settle cases outside the court, particularly when the strengths and weaknesses of a case become evident after documents have been exchanged between the

---

[6] See further Henry Brown and Arthur Marriott, op. cit., at p 40

[7] See S K Chatterjee, "Whether the Award of a Rent Review Tribunal is Admissible in Arbitration", 61 *Arbitration* (1995) 293

[8] See Professor David I Levine, "Early neutral evaluation: a follow-up report" in *Judicature* Vol 70 no 4 Dec–Jan 1987 and "Early Neutral Evaluation: The Second Phase", *Journal of Dispute Resolution*, Vol 1989 at p 1; see also Henry Brown and Arthur Marriott, op. cit., at p 41

parties to a dispute. Thus, both the English and the US systems follow similar practice in evaluating the strengths and weaknesses of a case.

3.5 PRIVATE JUDGING

In the United States, private judging is a process in certain states, such as California, New York, Ohio, Oregon and Texas, whereby the court refers cases to persons chosen by the parties. The system is otherwise known as *"rent a judge"*. This neutral judge is also known as a *"referee"* who must not be confused with a referee under the English court system. In certain special cases, that is, when parties cannot agree on the appointment of their referee, the court may appoint one. In Texas, it is obligatory that a referee must have successfully completed an approved alternative dispute resolution course of study. The concept of *"private judging"* is absent in England.

3.6 CONCLUSIONS

Alternative Dispute Resolution entails a variety of procedures; indeed, the United Stated seem to have adopted a number of procedures under the system *"multi-door courthouse"*, "high-low contracts", etc[9]. It is to be emphasised that whatever form of alternative dispute resolution may be adopted, it must be in accordance with the legal culture and environment of the country. The conceptual ideas such as "high-low contracts" or "multi-door courthouse" which are employed by certain courts in the United States, namely, the District of Columbia, must be considered seriously with reference to the current English judicial system before they are implemented. It is admitted that a shift from the adversarial system to the inquisitorial system is necessary, but the efficiency of the court system cannot be over-emphasised. The Alternative Dispute Resolution mechanism is based on the philosophy of friendly settlement of disputes in whatever form or form(s) it may adopt. The pre-requisite for operating a successful alternative dispute resolution system is to create an appropriate environment by informing the parties to a dispute of the advantages of it. The most important legal issue which deserves consideration is whether the alternative dispute resolution system is capable of protecting the legal rights of parties, offering remedies which the law under the court system cannot offer. This is not to say that ADR is inadequate in dealing with these issues; what is more important is whether ADR should be engaged in issues which may touch upon the constitutional rights of parties. ADR can provide a settlement on a mutually agreed basis but parties should be made aware of whether by so doing the alternative dispute resolution process requires them to compromise their rights. The alternative dispute resolution system operates on the perceived idea of how the court might have adjudged on the dispute; during the alternative dispute resolution the parties are informed of that but

[9] See further Henry Brown and Arthur Marriott, op. cit., at pp 443–46

the parties' inherent rights such as to seek remedies, for example, in the case of breach of contract, should not be taken away by a non-court system. Furthermore, can the alternative dispute resolution process provide, for example, injunctive relief or interim measures which are matters of fundamental rights of parties?

The alternative dispute resolution system of settling disputes is commendable if it is employed rationally and effectively. Parties will derive benefits from it, particularly in relation to time and costs. It is therefore crucial to consider what type or types of disputes may be referred to the alternative dispute resolution system. Apparently, disputes having a social dimension seem to be more readily settled by alternative dispute resolution system than disputes of a highly technical nature such as, shipping disputes or disputes relating to the protection of human rights. It is important for advocates of alternative dispute resolution to identify and inform clients or parties to a dispute of the deficiencies of the alternative dispute resolution system.

CHAPTER 4

Confidentiality in ADR

4.1 INTRODUCTION

One of the attractions of non-court proceedings or dispute settlement methods has been the confidentiality of the process. However, strictly speaking, in certain court proceedings confidentiality is also often maintained. If alternative dispute resolution parties specifically wish to maintain confidentiality, parties' wish in that regard must be maintained. Confidentiality in a family mediation is a very common phenomenon.

Privilege is different from confidentiality; they may overlap in maintaining confidentiality in respect of the same material, but either of them can exist without the other. Breach of confidentiality can give rise to a cause of action under English law as it amounts to a breach of confidence. The circumstances in which particular information is communicated may also impose an obligation on the defendant to maintain confidentiality[1]. The law of confidentiality is, in the final analysis, based on trust and when that confidence and trust are taken away there is a case for breach of confidentiality.

In alternative dispute resolution processes, confidentiality becomes extremely important. Whereas in court proceedings judges are in control of this issue, in the alternative dispute resolution process it falls on the parties to maintain this principle, and it is expected that a negotiator, a conciliator or mediator will strictly adhere to these principles.

4.2 CONFIDENTIALITY IN ADR

The importance of maintaining confidentiality in alternative dispute resolution has already been identified. The duty of confidentiality in the alternative dispute resolution process may arise by explicit agreement between the parties or by implication. Where, however, the subject-matter of a dispute is concerned with public policies issues and requires exposure to the public, the issue of confidentiality would not arise. Where the duty to maintain confidentiality has been made explicit by means of an agreement, a breach of that agreement may lead to a cause of action. But, unless the nature of a dispute relates to a public policy issue, the question remains whether there exists an implicit obligation to maintain confidentiality in the alternative dispute resolution process. The burden of maintaining confidentiality is very much on the person

[1] See further *Halsbury's Law of England*, 4th Edition, para 1455; see also *Frazer v Evans* [1969] 1 All ER p 8

who is conducting the alternative dispute resolution process. He or she has an additional duty to perform in that even though he or she may be in possession of certain confidential information in respect of both the parties that information should not prejudice his or her mind. There should not be any assumption on the part of a conciliator or a negotiator that he or she is authorised to disclose what has been discussed by the parties with him or her. Although in the United States, statutes and court rules, generally, include confidential information, in England, in the absence of any particular statute in this regard, problems of breach of confidentiality may easily be dealt with by applying the ordinary rules of the law of confidentiality.

The alternative dispute resolution systems contain an element of ethics which requires conciliators and mediators to maintain the principle of confidentiality, particularly in the interests of the parties concerned and also to maintain a respectable image for the system in general. Of course, specific rules of certain institutions may pay special attention to the issue of confidentiality, for example, the Code of Practice of the Family Mediators Association which attaches the principle of confidentiality, but which also maintains that the duty of confidentiality is excluded where disclosure may be required by the law. Of course, in such a situation no action for breach of confidentiality by the mediators may be brought by the parties. In *Frazer v Evans*[2] it was established that the test must be whether the public interest justifies the disclosure even though as a general rule a duty of confidentiality remains. The true test is whether there is a just cause for disclosure. Lord Denning, MR, stated that:

> *"There are some things which are of such public concern that the newspapers, the Press and indeed, everyone is entitled to make known the truth and to make fair comment on it. This is an integral part of the right of free speech and expression."*[3]

The issue of confidentiality is of utmost importance in the alternative dispute resolution system. A conciliator or mediator is thus required to choose between the conflicting duties of confidence and public interest[4] and should consider firstly whether in the public interest he has a duty to disclose any confidential information; and secondly whether there is any contractual provision restraining the disclosure but where the public interest may have an overriding effect. Perhaps the best course of action is to notify his position in regard to confidentiality to the parties, that is, why he feels that particular information must be disclosed.

---

[2] [1969] 1 QB 349

[3] op. cit., at 363

[4] Henry Brown and Arthur Marriott, op. cit., at p 359

4.3 PRIVILEGE

Privilege stands for the right of a person to withhold information from a judicial tribunal on a matter which it is adjudicating[5]. The reason for relying on privilege to withhold information is to protect the interests of the party which in the eyes of the law is more important than seeking the truth, and administration of justice. In England, the law recognises three classes of privilege: first, the exclusion of evidence on the grounds of public policy; second, the exclusion of certain information on the grounds of confidentiality; and third, the exclusion on the grounds that answering certain questions might tend to incriminate or expose a party to proceedings for a penalty[6]. In *D v NSPCC,* the House of Lords held that:

> *"... immunity from disclosure of their identity in civil proceedings should be extended to those who gave information about neglect or ill-treatment of children to a local authority or the N.S.P.C.C. to that which the law allowed to police informers, viz. that the identity of the informer might not be disclosed, whether by discovery, interrogatories, or questions at trial, the public interest served by preserving the anonymity of both classes of informants being analogous."*[7]

Of course, the onus is on the party concerned to prove that certain information is privileged. On this issue no distinction is maintained between public entities and individuals. The law of privilege against self-incrimination which was formulated by the Court of Appeal in *Blunt v Park Lane Hotel*[8] is not an absolute rule; it is subject to certain statutory exceptions such as section 14 of the Civil Evidence Act 1968. In *Blunt v Park Lane Hotel*, the Court of Appeal held that:

> *"It is only in proceedings for divorce on the ground of adultery that the spouse will be protected from answering interrogatories if the answers might tend to prove the adultery ..."*[9]

Section 14 of the Civil Evidence Act, 1968 provides that:

> *(1) The right of a person in any legal proceedings other than criminal proceedings to refuse to answer any question or produce any document or thing if to do so would tend to expose that person to proceedings for an offence or for the recovery of a penalty-*
>
> *(a) shall apply only as regards criminal offences under the law of any part of the United Kingdom and penalties provided for by such law; and*

---

[5] Colin Tapper, *Cross and Tapper on Evidence*, LexisNexis UK (2003)

[6] *D v NSPCC* [1977] 2 W.L.R. at p 201

[7] op. cit., at 201

[8] [1942] 2 KB 253 at 257

[9] op. cit., at 257

(b) *shall include a like right to refuse to answer any question or produce any document or thing if to do so would tend to expose the husband or wife of that person to proceedings for any such criminal offence or for the recovery of any such penalty.*

(2) *In so far as any existing enactment conferring (in whatever words) powers of inspection or investigation confers on a person (in whatever words) any right otherwise than in criminal proceedings to refuse to answer any question or give any evidence tending to incriminate that person, subsection (1) above shall apply to that right as it applies to the right described in that subsection; and every such existing enactment shall be construed accordingly.*

(3) *In so far as any existing enactment provides (in whatever words) that in any proceedings other than criminal proceedings a person shall not be excused from answering any question or giving any evidence on the ground that to do so may incriminate that person, that enactment shall be construed as providing also that in such proceedings a person shall not be excused from answering any question or giving any evidence on the ground that to do so may incriminate the husband or wife of that person*

(4) *Where any existing enactment (however worded) that-*

(a) *confers powers of inspection or investigation; or*

(b) *provides as mentioned in subsection (3) above, further provides (in whatever words) that any answer or evidence given by a person shall not be admissible in evidence against that person in any proceedings or class of proceedings (however described, and whether criminal or not), that enactment shall be construed as providing also that any answer or evidence given by that person shall not be admissible in evidence against the husband or wife of that person in the proceedings or class of proceedings in question.*

(5) *In this section "existing enactment" means any enactment passed before this Act; and the references to giving evidence are references to giving evidence in any manner, whether by furnishing information, making discovery, producing documents or otherwise."*

In this connection, it would be apposite to briefly discuss the legal aspects of *"professional privilege"*.

4.3.1 Professional Privilege

According to the age-old rule which was developed by the court in *McGowan v Wright*[10], communications between a professional legal adviser and his clients are privileged. However, such communications must be made for

---

[10] (1852) 15 D 229

professional purposes and when a professional relationship subsists[11]. In *Crompton (Alfred) Amusement Machines Ltd v Customs & Excise Commissioners*[12] it was decided that communications made to all by a litigant or his legal advisor to a third party may be regarded as privileged only if made in contemplation of legal issues. If the privilege is validly claimed, its continuity may not be questioned[13]. On the other hand, a privilege may be waived expressly or by implication.

In *Guinness Peat Properties Ltd v Fitzroy Robinson Partnership (a firm)*[14] it was decided that privilege attached to a document may be lost by an inadvertent disclosure on inspection.

Statements made on a "without prejudice" basis also attract the status of privileged information. Law in England and Wales encourages negotiation on a "without prejudice" basis in order to minimise recourse to court proceedings. In *Cutts v Head*, Oliver, LJ, said:

> *"That the rule rests, at least in part, upon public policy is clear from many authorities, and the convenient starting point of the inquiry is the nature of the underlying policy. It is that parties should be encouraged so far as possible to settle their disputes without resort to litigation and should not be discouraged by the knowledge that anything that is said in the course of such negotiations (and that includes, of course, as much the failure to reply to an offer as an actual reply) may be used to their prejudice in the course of the proceedings."*[15].

Mere use of the term "without prejudice" does not necessarily make the contents of the relevant document privileged. The test is whether or not communications are actually directed towards reaching a settlement[16]. It is worth reproducing the principles laid down by the House of Lords in regard to "without prejudice" in *Rush & Tomkins*[17]. In this case, the second defendants sought disclosure by the plaintiff of a *"without prejudice"* correspondence. The plaintiffs conceded that the correspondence might be relevant to the issues between them, but refused to disclose its contents on the grounds that it was privileged. The second defendants applied for an order for specific discovery. The House of Lords held that:

> *"... in general the "without prejudice" rule made inadmissible in any subsequent litigation concerned with the same subject matter proof of any*

---

11 *Balabel v Air India* [1988] 1 Ch at 317

12 [1972] 2 QB at 102

13 *The Aegis Blaze* [1986] 1 Lloyd's Rep, Court of Appeal, at 203

14 [1987] 2 All ER 716 at 729

15 *Cutts v Head* [1984] Ch 290 at 306

16 *Rush & Tomkins Ltd v Greater London Council & Another* [1989] 1 A.C. 1280; *Tomlin v Standard Telephones* [1969] 1 W.L.R. 1378; Walker v Wilsher (1889) 23 QBD 335

17 [1989] AC 1280; see also *Parry v New Group Newspapers Ltd* (1990) 140 *New Law Journal* 1719

> *admissions made with a genuine intention to reach a settlement; and that admissions made to reach settlement with a different party within the same litigation were also inadmissible whether or not settlement was reached with that party."*
>
> *"... the general public policy that applied to protect genuine negotiations from being admissible in evidence also applied to protect those negotiations from being disclosed to third parties ..."*[18]

The time of claiming privilege is extremely important in the alternative dispute resolution system in any of its forms, but on the other hand, extensive use of privilege might hinder the progress of settling disputes by ADR. What is most important is not to disclose some of the information to a third party which has been discussed in the settlement process. Of course, privilege on the grounds of public policy may also be used in the alternative dispute resolution system, but the exceptions to a "without prejudice" information are also applicable to ADR. In *Rush & Tomkins Ltd v Greater London Council*, Lord Griffiths stated, inter alia, that:

> *"Nearly all these cases in which the scope of the 'without prejudice' rule has been considered concern the admissibility of evidence at trial after negotiations have failed. In such circumstances no question of discovery arises because the parties are well aware of what passed between them in the negotiations. These cases show that the rule is not absolute and resort may be had to the 'without prejudice' material for a variety of reasons when the justice of the case requires it ... the underlying purpose of the rule which is to protect a litigant from being embarrassed by any admission made purely in an attempt to achieve a settlement."*[19]

In claiming privilege in regard of disclosure of information, the primary ethos of alternative dispute resolution should not be defeated. Unnecessary privileges will simply hinder the use of the alternative dispute resolution.

In England, a statute may provide for conciliation as a method of settling disputes, see for example, sections 133 and 134 of The Employment Protection (Consolidation) Act 1978, section 10 of The Contempt of Court Act 1981, and Practice Directions (Family Division Conciliation Procedure) (Nos 1 and 2) [1982] 1 W.L.R. 1420 and [1984] 1 W.L.R. 1326.

There still persists controversy whether an entire ADR system or any element of it should be privileged or not, but there does not seem to exist any controversy that the information disclosed during an alternative dispute resolution system must remain privileged. There does not exist any legislation on the issue of whether an entire alternative dispute resolution system should be privileged and, if so, on what grounds. The Law Commission's Inquiry

[18] op. cit., at 1280

[19] op. cit., at 1300

maintained that privilege attaches to communication between spouses with a view to reconciliation. The legal position in England on this issue still remains uncertain. However, privilege, if any, attaches to the parties and not to the person in charge of alternative dispute resolution, although according to some, privilege in family mediation should attach to a mediator[20].

The crucial legal issue to consider is whether people conducting alternative dispute resolution are to be treated as arbitrators. Under the Arbitration Act 1996 arbitrators are allowed privileges and immunities; unless the status of people conducting alternative dispute resolution is clearly determined, the issue of privileges and immunities may not be clarified.

4.4 CONCLUSIONS

There is no doubt that confidentiality in the alternative dispute resolution system should be maintained in respect of certain disputes, namely, matrimonial or protection of children or other similar matters, and that the settled agreement under ADR should remain confidential. The issue of confidentiality is one which must be determined by the parties themselves. But, generally the proceedings must be conducted in confidence. In arbitrations the award of a tribunal may be published with the consent of parties. There is no reason why the same system may not be applied to commercial disputes settled by ADR. The issue of confidentiality in respect of matrimonial matters or child-molestation matters should be considered on a separate footing.

As stated earlier, seeking too much privilege might defeat the purposes of alternative dispute resolution. There does not seem to be any real reason why commercial disputes settled by ADR may not be published with the consent of parties. Publication of settled disputes might encourage the commercial world to refer its disputes to the ADR system.

[20] D Parker and A Parkinson, "Solicitors and Family Conciliation Service: A Basis for Professional Co-operation" (1985) 15 *Family Law* at 270

CHAPTER 5

The Duty to Advise a Client to Consider ADR and the Limits to that Duty

5.1 INTRODUCTION

A duty to advise a client as to the propriety of ADR would not arise until the client has approached a lawyer with a dispute. As usual, the initial duty of the lawyer would be to listen to the client, particularly by making him as comfortable as possible. The lawyer must not be overpowering, impatient and must be prepared to listen even to unstructured statements made by his client. When necessary, the lawyer must look up the relevant documentary evidence. Usually clients have pre-conceived ideas that litigation would be the best method of resolving their dispute. While listening to a client the lawyer must consider whether the dispute is suitable for the ADR system or for court proceedings. He or she must not unnecessarily divert the dispute into either the ADR method or court proceedings. It is at this stage that a lawyer has a duty to clarify to his/her client the comparative risks, costs, tactical approaches and the probable results between the ADR system and court proceedings, in particular by pointing out the issue of enforcement if the ADR system is pursued.

The purpose of this chapter is to point out the legal duties of a lawyer and the extent to which he/she should apply the principle of that duty of care and skill in advising his/her client. Under no circumstances shall a lawyer mislead his/her client nor would he/she do anything for personal interest.

5.2 THE DUTY OF THE CLIENT

The client must make a full disclosure of the facts and a skilful lawyer should know how to warn a client as to consequences of non-disclosure. Often a client does not make disclosure of facts in the belief they would not be relevant to his case. A lawyer should make clear to his/her client the importance of making of what is known as a *"clean breast statement"*; hence the need for skill on the part of the lawyer to create and maintain a friendly environment while holding a conference and checking periodically with his/her client whether all facts have been disclosed. A prudent lawyer should point out diplomatically to his/her client the consequences of providing misleading or untrue information. On the other hand, it must be borne in mind that it is the client who knows his case best. Unless all facts have been disclosed, it is inconceivable that a lawyer would be able to identify the nature of the dispute and the legal issues thereto in order to be able to advise his client whether his case is fit for the ADR method or court proceedings.

If a dispute appears to be primarily fact-based rather than a proper legal dispute, the lawyer should advise his/her client not to think in terms of court proceedings but instead in terms of settlement by conciliation. In addition, he/she should point out how the results reached by a conciliation process may have legal effect or whether they will have any legal effect at all.

Therefore, on the one hand, the lawyer cannot afford to be unfriendly to his client nor can he create any kind of bad impression upon his/her client, but at the same time, he must try to seek the truth. Sometimes it proves to be useful to ask a client to submit a written statement of his dispute. This system also provides a lawyer with an opportunity to refer to the document which is as good as an unofficial witness statement.

It is suggested that lawyers should adopt a procedure whereby clients are also clear as to the scope of their obligations and functions, in particular, disclosure of facts and cooperation. It is therefore re-emphasised that during the initial stage, a prudent lawyer should directly point out to his/her client the importance of making full disclosure of facts with evidence where possible.

5.3 A LAWYER'S DUTY TO JUSTIFY THE PROPRIETY OF THE ADR SYSTEM

Under the Commercial Court and the High Court Practice Directions, an advising lawyer is required to draw to the attention of his/her client the possibility of settling a dispute by means of ADR. The Practice Directions of the High Court are now briefly discussed.

One of the important Practice Directions which was issued by the Family Division of the High Court on 2 November 1982, came into force on 1 January 1983[1]. The Principal Registry of the Family Division set up a pilot scheme of conciliation in contested applications in matrimonial proceedings for custody, access and variation thereof. In addition to saving time and expenses both to the parties and the Court, the object of the scheme was to *"give an opportunity for agreement to be reached without the bitterness and exchange of recriminations which often develops between the parties when these issues remain in dispute."*[2] The Practice Direction emphasised that no affidavit should be filed or exchanged until after conciliation failed or until the Registrar so directed.

In order to facilitate conciliation, soon after an application is lodged, arrangements would be made for a Registrar to attend to the application along with a court welfare officer. Both the parties and any legal advisers having conduct of the case would be required to attend. As to the procedure, the Practice Direction stated that:

---

[1] Practice Direction published in [1982] 1 WLR at 1420.

[2] op. cit., at 1420–21

> *"The nature of the application and the matters in dispute will be outlined to the registrar and the welfare officer. If the dispute continues, the parties and their advisers will be given the opportunity of retiring to a private room together with the welfare officer to attempt to reach agreement. The discussion will be privileged and will not be disclosed on any subsequent application. Anything which is said before the registrar on such appointments will also remain privileged."*[3]

If the conciliation appointment is successful, the Registrar will make such orders as are agreed between the parties. In the event of the application not being successful, any subsequent application which may be made to the Registrar will be dealt with by a different Registrar and a court welfare officer. *"Applications for variation of custody or access orders made as a result of conciliation will be generally dealt with by the same Registrar who dealt with the initial conciliation appointment."*[4]

In the event of the conciliation appointment being unsuccessful the Registrar will give such direction as he deems appropriate in regard to the obtaining of welfare officer's reports and the lodging of affidavits.

In 1984, by the Practice Direction (Family Division: Conciliation Procedure) (No. 2)[5], the 1982 scheme was extended to include s. 41 applications referred by a judge to a Registrar for further inquiry. The scheme was further extended to include contested applications for custody and access in guardianship proceedings and for care and control and access in certain wardship proceedings, other than those in which a local authority is involved. In wardship and guardianship proceedings, it is for the Registrar to consider whether the matter is appropriate for inclusion in the conciliation list either on the first appointment or subsequently.

An important difference between the 1982 Practice Direction and the 1984 Practice Direction is that whereas the former provided that children aged 11 years or over should be brought to the conciliation appointment, the latter lowered the age to 9 years for that purpose. Furthermore, according to the later Practice Direction, *"if only one of two or more children is above the age of 9 years the younger child or children may also attend."*[6] This Practice Direction also emphasised the importance of making application to the clerk to the registrar to vacate conciliation appointments as soon as possible.

The Practice Direction *"Ancillary Relief Procedure – Pilot Scheme"* dated 16 June 1997[7] was replaced by the *Practice Direction dated 25 May 2000*[8]. This latter Practice Direction made it clear that the existing *"pilot scheme"* rules in

[3] op. cit., at 1421

[4] ibid.,

[5] This was published in [1984] WLR 1326

[6] ibid.,

[7] See [1977] 3 ALL ER 768

[8] Reproduced in [2000] 3 ALL ER 379

relation to ancillary relief, which applied in specified courts would become, with significant revisions, of general application. The new procedure was intended to reduce delay, facilitate settlements, minimise legal costs, and to provide the court with greater effective control over the conduct of the proceedings. The *"Pre-application Protocol"* annexed to this Direction details the steps the parties should take to seek and provide information from and to each other prior to the commencement of any ancillary relief application.

The new procedure is primarily concerned with the Financial Dispute Resolution (FDR) appointment. The FDR appointment "is to be treated as a meeting held for the purposes of discussion and negotiation. Such meetings which were previously held for the purposes of conciliation have been developed as a means of reducing the tension which inevitably arises in matrimonial and family disputes and facilitating settlement of those disputes."[9] Although the Pre-Application Protocol does not directly use the terms alternative dispute resolution, it is maintained that it contains most of the attributes and purposes of ADR.

Thus, it is relevant to be familiar with this Protocol. The Practice Direction clearly states that parties must approach FDR appointments openly and without reserve. Confidentiality of the contents of FDR meetings is given high priority by this Practice Direction. Any statement made by parties during an FDR appointment will not be admissible in evidence except *"at the trial of a person for an offence committed at the appointment or in the very exceptional circumstances indicated in Re D."*[10]

Courts will expect parties to make offers and proposals and to give them proper consideration. The legal representatives attending FDR appointments should have full knowledge of the cases. Unnecessary use of experts will be restricted by the Court. Parties are encouraged to agree on a single expert who may be instructed jointly by them. Where parties are unable to agree on an expert, the Court may use its powers under Part 35 of the Civil Procedure Rules to direct that evidence be given by one expert only. It is deemed appropriate now to briefly discuss the *Pre-application Protocol.*

The origins of the Pre-application Protocol may be found in the Woolf Report—*Access to Justice* published in 1996. The Pre-application Protocol was agreed by the Lord Chancellor's Ancillary Relief Advisory Committee in April, 2000. The aim of the Pre-application Protocol is to ensure that:

> *"(a) pre-application disclosure and negotiation takes place in appropriate cases; (b) where there is pre-application disclosure and negotiation, it is dealt with: (i) cost effectively; (ii) in line with the overriding objectives of the Family Proceedings (Amendment No. 2) Rules 1999; (c) the parties are in a position to settle the case fairly and early without litigation."*

[9] ibid.,

[10] ibid., see also *Re D (Minor) (Conciliation: disclosure of information)* [1993] 2 ALL ER 693

In so far as the High Court (Queen's Bench Division and Chancery Division) is concerned in 1994, Creswell J (Commercial Court) encouraged parties to consider the use of alternative dispute resolution (ADR), namely, conciliation and mediation, as a means of settling their disputes[11]. Although judges will not participate as conciliators or mediators, in appropriate cases they may invite parties to consider these alternative dispute resolution methods, particularly where the cost of litigation would be disproportionate to the claim.

The Clerk to the Commercial Court maintains a list of individuals and bodies offering ADR services. The Judge also pointed out that although the Commercial Court will render its traditional services, legal advisers should inform their clients of the most cost effective means of settling their disputes.

On 24 January 1995, Lord Taylor of Gosforth L.J. gave another Practice Direction[12] reminding practitioners of their duty to conduct cases economically; otherwise, they will be liable for order for costs, including wasted costs orders.

The text of this Practice Note has been reproduced in Annex 1 and 2.

Under the High Court Practice Direction a lawyer in the conduct of the matter is required to lodge with the court at least 2 months before the trial a check list containing answers to various questions, including questioning whether the possibility of using ADR was put to the parties and explored. But the fact remains that the ADR process not being mandatory may not, ultimately, settle a dispute.

However, a responsible lawyer has the obligation to provide full advice on ADR to his own Client, and in so advising the legal and financial implications of the ADR method and court proceedings must be fully discussed. The lawyer must then seek the decision of his client as to which course he or she would like to take. In advising a client on the use of ADR, the weaknesses of the ADR system as well as its strengths must be clearly pointed out.

Currently, a lawyer's duty seems to be confined to the issue whether he or she discussed the possibility of the use of ADR; whether it will actually be used or not will very much depend on the decision of the parties concerned. Here a prudent lawyer should be careful that in advising his clients he does not show any bias in favour or against ADR or court proceedings.

The lawyer has a particular duty to draw the attention of his client to the cost effectiveness of both ADR and court proceedings, in addition to pointing out the prospect of winning or losing in court proceedings. A lawyer has also the ethical duty of pointing out the amount of his fees if the dispute is referred to ADR or to the court proceedings.

5.4 MEDIATION

One of the conditions of mediation is that all parties must agree to participate in the mediation process. In the absence of any voluntary consent of the parties

[11] See the Practice Note published in [1994] 1 ALL ER 34

[12] See the Practice Note published in [1995] 1 ALL ER 385

the mediation cannot be a proper one as the acceptability of the mediation will always be suspect. Mediators should be selected in the light of the nature of the disputes and the issues involved in it. A mediator may be selected either through an ADR institution or through nomination by the parties. Mediators nominated by the parties command respect and trust of the parties but this is not to suggest that mediators selected through an ADR organisation will not command the same trust of the parties. ADR organisations have the advantage of knowing the quality and ability of mediators and parties will have the choice of choosing one from a probable few.

Mediators must have the knowledge and expertise in the subject matter of a dispute as well as mediation skills; the latter is as important as the former. In fact, the training and experience of a mediator combined with his amiability, his understanding and approach to a problem are very important qualities for being a mediator.

A mediator takes a facilitative approach and he must not try to dominate the mediation process. Parties must be allowed to participate and present their ideas and he must have knowledge of case management. The best mediator is he who can combine mediation skills with subject matter expertise. Mediators should have inter-disciplinary knowledge as often many disputes require such knowledge but at no stage during the process should a mediator lose the confidence of the parties. The mediator must remain approachable to the parties at all times during the mediation process. A mediator must be like a friend to the parties and at the same time an expert who by virtue of his knowledge and skills commands trust and confidence of the parties. There is a danger in appointing only experts on the subject matter in dispute; mediation skills must be combined with the expertise.

Where however the subject matter of a dispute is complex and / or multi-dimensional, more than one mediator may be appointed. It is important to ensure that in such situations mediators can work together in the interest of the parties.

A mediator must be prepared to maintain a flexible approach to dispute resolution and always be mindful that the parties' interests are protected. In order to make mediation a successful and speedy process, it is important that the scope of the mediation is determined by asking the parties the questions with which the mediation would be concerned, and that an agreement in writing determines the limits of mediation.

Costs of mediation entail the mediator's fees, legal costs and other expenses which will be borne by the parties. Other expenses in this context are expenses for hiring the place for mediation, obtaining the services from the institution concerned and the accommodation of mediators, if necessary. In this sense there is hardly any difference between the holding of an arbitration and mediation.

In the event of a party failing to afford the cost of mediation or being reluctant to pay the costs, the other party may pay all the fees. This kind of situation directly gives the impression that mediation might not succeed in that the party not paying the fees is not interested in the mediation. There is therefore reason for minimising the costs of mediation so that the parties may be persuaded to refer their dispute to mediation. The purpose of mediating a dispute would be defeated if it becomes unnecessarily prolonged as costs mount and confidence of the parties may be lost. Mediation therefore should be less time consuming, less cost-orientated and different from court proceedings and arbitral proceedings. The issue of cost is even more important because legal aid is not allowed to mediation.

5.5 IS THERE ANY DUTY TO USE ADR SYSTEM?

ADR is not mandatory, but there is no harm in the appointed lawyers advising clients by discussing the range of ADR methods available, the nature of the outcome, time-scale and the finance involved. In pointing out the option of using ADR, legal advisers should also inform their clients of the advantages and disadvantages of using an ADR system compared to those of court proceedings. A legal adviser is therefore required to maintain his integrity and advise his clients of their best interests. On the other hand, as stated earlier, ADR is a system which offers various options and can be used at any stage of a dispute; being mindful of the interests of their clients, lawyers will always try to settle disputes by mutual agreement which, in many ways, is an aspect of the ADR process.

Negotiated settlement has always been a common phenomenon in large claims, particularly in respect of the construction industry or utility industry. Whether it was called ADR or not, the negotiated settlement system has a long history; whereas in the United States the system is much more consolidated and identifiable, in the United Kingdom it is still in its infancy. One of the recent examples of using the negotiated settlement system in the United Kingdom was in respect of the Channel Tunnel Dispute. There is no reason why a negotiated settlement system may not be extended to include all other types of dispute, provided a system of effective enforcement is devised and implemented. Of course, in respect of child care and matrimonial disputes, a negotiated settlement has become quite popular. ADR can be made compulsory by parties' agreement when a clause to that effect is incorporated into the contract. There are two factors which should be considered in making ADR compulsory by legislation:

(a) the perception of parties involved in a dispute, that is, from a psychological standpoints often they would prefer a coercive decision-making such as decision-making through court proceedings;

(b) the enforcement issue.

As stated earlier, if ADR is adopted by the parties as their dispute settlement method and if a party is in breach of an agreed settlement, then there is a case for a breach of contract and in that event the usual court procedure should take care of it. ADR can be used at any stage in the proceedings or even before initiating any legal proceedings. The purpose is to avoid legal costs and time, in addition to minimising the psychological distress of the parties. It is therefore an incumbent duty of lawyers to advise their clients whether a non-litigation procedure might be more useful and less expensive. This advice should be given at the earliest stage and if no legal proceedings have been instituted then the ADR process can be introduced.

5.6 ASSESSMENT OF RISKS

ADR authors tend to emphasise the issue of the risk assessment and in their opinion, the parties must be told of the degree of risk involved, both financial and otherwise. If a negotiated settlement is not reached, any good legal practitioner must advise his or her clients of the risks involved in any proceedings[13], whether court proceedings or ADR proceedings. It is for the lawyer to ensure that any proceedings are based on hard legal issues and that the client's interests will be protected and that the client will not be subject to unnecessary legal costs.

All competent lawyers should carry out risk assessment in regard to a case. This entails assessment of the legal issues and also the assessment of prospects of vindicating the parties' rights. Cost analysis is part of this exercise and a client should be informed in sufficient time of the projected legal costs so that he does not get any surprises at a later stage. From this standpoint, the difference between ADR proceedings and court proceedings seem to be minimal.

Furthermore, it has been emphasised earlier that even during proceedings thoughtful lawyers should always try to negotiate an amicable settlement, when possible. Case management is a term which is often used in relation to a judge's capacity to manage a case in a courtroom but all lawyers must have competence in case management too. During the proceedings, clients should also be notified on a regular basis by lawyers of the potential costs for future stages.

It is to be borne in mind that direct negotiations between parties often prove to be unsuccessful and therefore proposals for negotiation must be put forward to the parties through the lawyers, and this method entails costs.

Before advising a client to be involved in an ADR process, two criteria must be satisfied:

(a) risk assessment, and

(b) the prospect of successfully concluding a negotiated settlement quickly.

[13] K Mackie, D Miles, W Marsh, op. cit., at 61-64

As to the second criterion, it must be ensured that sufficient information is already available and that the client has a strong position in a dispute. It must also be considered whether intervention by a third party, that is, through the ADR process, might prove to be effective. It might be an idea to ascertain through the lawyers whether the parties are reluctant to go into the court, and if they are, then a significant part of the battle is over. ADR might prove to be very effective for corporate bodies facing legal claims.

Where however a straightforward summary judgement may be available there is no need to initiate the ADR system. A lawyer should also point out to a client that ADR may not be the most appropriate process to settle the dispute where the party is adopting a delaying tactic or where there will be no real saving of costs and where parties' legal position is not strong enough. In a complex case, the lawyer advising his client must be able to comprehend the complex legal issues and indicate the prospects of success in percentage terms where using the ADR process or by court proceedings.

On the other hand, parties might like to use the ADR system for assessing their legal position even before they decide to go to the court of law. Even in that case the parties should be advised of the legal costs in the process and assured of confidentiality on a "without prejudice" basis.

The presumed benefits of ADR are low cost, speed, and control over the case. They may not be confirmed if ADR is commenced at a premature stage, that is, the basic issues involved in a dispute have not been properly identified. One should not encourage ADR unless one has collected all the information relating to a case and one can see that the parties are willing to compromise and that there will be a real cost difference between court proceedings and the ADR system, if activated. ADR might be very welcome by parties when they are not willing to disclose their matters in public in court proceedings.

The ADR system should be adopted as a preliminary stage for avoiding court proceedings but some of the elements of the court proceedings are also useful for the ADR process in order to avoid the risk, namely, disclosure of all information including technical information by experts, if necessary. This is also known as a "*cards on the table approach*".[14] Of course, this is done on a "*without prejudice*" basis. Incidentally, prudent Counsel, before being involved in court proceedings does the same. This is the process whereby parties are alerted as to their strong and weak points and whereby risks are identified. All dispute settlement procedures, in fact, should do this. If information is divulged on a "*without prejudice*" basis there is no reason why parties should not co-operate in finding a solution to their disputes and avoid costs of litigation. The difficulty remains, of course, that under the ADR process there is no obligation to disclose; in court proceedings orders can be obtained for compulsory disclosures. But in the interests of parties it is only advisable that they disclose all information for an evaluation of their claims and settle it

[14] K Mackie, D Miles, W Marsh, op. cit., at 72

through the ADR process. A tactful party should volunteer to disclose all information. Parties should appreciate that once a dispute has been negotiated a settlement might be transformed into a legally binding instrument. Furthermore, instead of using ADR as a delaying tactic, parties should take it seriously in order to identify their respective strengths and weaknesses. A half-hearted approach to ADR should not be adopted. Eventually, it will provide to be more expensive than court proceedings.

If one thinks of court proceedings seriously, prudent common sense will also try to identify the weaknesses and strengths of a case and there is no reason why the parties should not volunteer to be aware of their strengths and weaknesses in an informal setting and settle their dispute amicably. It is emphasised that the success of ADR very much depends on the perception of the parties towards ADR.

Risk assessment in this context means two things:

(a) that through their submission the parties would like to know their respective positions in their case, and in order to determine their precise position the full disclosure of all events would be necessary; and

(b) in the event of any non-disclosure the parties create their own risk themselves in that if they are prepared to go to court without properly assessing their risks, they will know the outcome only after incurring high legal costs.

5.7 LIMITS TO MEDIATION

There are certain limits to mediation and these limits are set primarily by the nature of a dispute or the urgency with which the dispute needs to be settled. It is therefore possible to categorise generally the types of dispute that may not be suitable for settlement by mediation:

(a) where immediate injunctive relief or conservatory measures are necessary;

(b) where enforcement of a document is necessary through the court procedures, and the subject-matter of a dispute relates to the enforcement of the document in a particular jurisdiction;

(c) where in order to satisfy a limitation period proceedings must be instituted because a reference to mediation might cross the time-period;

(d) where issues of constitutional and fundamental rights are involved;

(e) corporate insolvency or individual bankruptcy;

(f) criminal actions, fiscal matters, intellectual property matters but not damages recoverable from breach of such rights;

(g) inheritance and succession matters; and

(h) fundamental rights including a right to seek asylum.

Of course, like arbitration, in mediation the party autonomy rule prevails, and the parties may be opposed to mediation. There is no machinery as yet except in family related issues whereby the parties are obliged to go through a mediation process prior to referring a dispute to a court of law.

Lack of faith in the mediation process can operate as a limit to offering mediation as a means of settling disputes. In other words, psychological conceptions may operate as barriers to mediation. Furthermore, if a contract provides for arbitration or court proceedings as the means of settling disputes arising under that contract, unless the parties by means of a compromise reverse their contractual obligations and decide to refer their dispute to a mediation process, mediation cannot be activated.

5.8 CONCLUSIONS

Mediation is a thoroughly voluntary process of settling disputes in that the parties must voluntarily agree except by agreed terms but where the terms are not agreed upon they can abandon mediation. There thus exist two legal situations in a mediation process:

(a) where terms are agreed and drafted and signed by both the parties there is no reason why the agreed terms may not have any contractual force[15];

(b) should the parties fail to agree on any terms then there is no binding element in mediation; the mediation process is, in effect, frustrated.

In a mediation process the mediator assists the parties in reaching their own decision, but he is not a decision-maker. A mediator "*facilitates*" mediation in that he assists the parties in clarifying issues and helps each side to understand the other's perspective. This aspect of mediation is usually known as facilitating mediation. Where a mediator evaluates a dispute, which is a non-binding assessment, it is for the parties either to accept or reject that evaluation. This type of mediation is known as evaluative mediation. It is to be pointed out, however, that if what is initially a non-binding assessment of a dispute is accepted by the parties and they agree to the terms and conditions of a settlement then an evaluative mediation gives rise to a binding mediation because the parties have agreed to the outcome of the settlement.

In a mediation process parties do not transfer the decision-making power to the mediator; they simply authorise the mediator to control the mediation

[15] This point has been further developed in chapter 11.

process, and the control mechanism entails clarification of issues and management of mediation process. Whereas in an arbitration procedure, an arbitrator gives his considered views, in the mediation process the parties may reach an agreed conclusion by themselves with the help of the mediator in his capacity of an advisor.

A lawyer's duty to advise his clients to consider ADR as a dispute settlement system is a tricky one. He must not unduly persuade his client to refer his dispute to ADR, nor can he encourage him to enter into court proceedings knowing its limitations. In this dilemma, his own financial benefits, as fees, be it for participating in the ADR system or the court proceedings, must not be a determining factor. A lawyer is also required to adhere to the Practice Directions issued by the High Court.

On the other hand, being familiar with the weaknesses of the ADR system, particularly in regard to the enforcement of the agreed solution, he has a duty to draw the attention of his client to his factor. This is an issue which must be considered by both the parties, in consultation with their lawyers, in order to attain the best benefit for themselves.

Risk assessment and costs are other important elements to be considered in advising a client whether or not to refer a dispute to ADR.

CHAPTER 6

Representation of Parties at Non-adjudicatory ADR

6.1 INTRODUCTION

Representations on behalf of the parties of non-adjudicatory alternative dispute resolution system require a special skill on the part of the representatives acting on behalf of the parties. ADR is predominantly supposed to work in a non-legal environment; therefore, the characteristics of and skills required by representatives of non-adjudicatory processes are very different from those that are required by legal representatives in ordinary judicial proceedings. The common element that may be identified in both systems is the power and skills of presenting arguments on behalf of the parties. Therefore, the caution must be entered that a legal environment is not created in a non-adjudicatory alternative dispute resolution system. No adversarial climate must be allowed to be created as it might escalate the differences between the parties. The purpose of such a system is to seek solutions which are mutually beneficial and which would narrow the gap between the parties.

In this chapter an attempt is made to discuss an advocate's strategies and functions when he/she is required to participate in a non-adjudicatory alternative dispute resolution system.

6.2 REPRESENTATION OF PARTIES AT A NON-ADJUDICATORY ADR

It is important that parties feel at ease with their representatives. Parties usually know their case best; they may not understand the technicalities and strategies involved in their case, but it is the representative acting on behalf of each party who must have a thorough knowledge of the facts of the case; otherwise, the party concerned will not have any confidence in him/her. On the other hand, each party must make a full disclosure of the facts, otherwise its representative will be misrepresenting the case on behalf of its client. Both the parties and their representatives must also create a friendly environment, and the representative must not only be a person of skills and knowledge, but also he/she must be tolerant and helpful.

However difficult and technical a case might be, a representative must not use jargon which his/her client will find difficult to understand.

The parties also must be understanding in that, they should realise or appreciate the strengths and weaknesses in their respective case. It is also important for parties to appreciate that it usually takes two to make a quarrel, which may be based on misunderstanding of the terms in a contract, or because of some unacceptable conduct on their part. It is also extremely important that parties fully co-operate with their representatives.

6.3 THE ADVOCATE'S FUNCTIONS

An advocate's function is to advocate the cause of his client; in a non-adjudicatory alternative dispute resolution system an advocate must restrain himself or herself from becoming formalistic, intimidating and unduly legalistic. He or she must be capable of explaining issues and problems in a simple and correct manner without using jargon. He or she must appreciate that settling disputes is a non-adjudicatory process; references to law should be kept to a minimum. He or she must appear to be a friendly and amiable person in whom parties can place confidence and who would be regarded as a friend rather than an adversary.

Lawyers should not have any pre-conceived ideas that their experience in the courtroom environment would help them. He or she should behave himself or herself predominantly as a non-lawyer; but this is where the problem lies in that many lawyers instead of simplifying issues tend to complicate them and are unable to explain legal issues in a simple way by using simple language. An advocate's success in a non-adjudicatory alternative dispute resolution or even in a courtroom environment depends on how clearly he or she presents the case on behalf of his or her client and thus the client also will not have any doubt as to what the alternative dispute resolution system or court proceedings were deliberating on his or her behalf. This is one of the most important criteria of good advocacy.

Before accepting an appointment as an advocate for a non-adjudicatory or even an adjudicatory alternative dispute resolution system, an advocate must acquaint himself or herself with the procedural details and the philosophy of the system in which he or she will be working[1].

Depending upon the nature of a dispute the participation of the advocate would vary, for example, in commercial conciliation or conciliation of a dispute of a technical nature, such as construction or engineering, the advocate is required to assemble documents, hold conferences and prepare written submissions; but in family mediations solicitors usually advise the clients outside, instead of at the actual mediation forum. Whatever may be the nature of a dispute in a non-adjudicatory ADR an advocate can never be legalistic, formalistic and behave himself or herself in a manner which would create the environment of an adversarial judicial system.

[1] Henry Brown and Arthur Marriott, op. cit., at p 300

It is crucial that an advocate has a thorough understanding of ADR in preparing his or her case. Brown and Marriott identify the following points as guidelines for the understanding and preparation of a case by an advocate in non-adjudicatory ADR:

(a) An advocate should understand what kind of ADR would be suitable for the case paying attention to the nature of the dispute, and the time that may be allocated to reaching a solution;

(b) After the process has been chosen written submissions are to be prepared by an advocate;

(c) An advocate is required to understand the facts of the case and the documents in order to be able to isolate the important issues, the strengths, weakness and the strategies;

(d) In civil or commercial ADR, a lawyer is usually required to make a presentation of his/her client's case to a neutral adviser, and the success of that presentation depends on his or her understanding of the case demonstrated at a formal hearing. He or she must understand that it would be essential for him or her to highlight cogently and rationally the main issues over a short period of time; "beating around the bush" would defeat the purpose.

(e) In the process of presentation and submission a competent and effective advocate must be able to convince the other side that his or her client's case is meritorious and is highly likely to succeed in a trial if ADR does not lead to an acceptable settlement. Therefore, an advocate is required to maximise the prospect of obtaining a positive evaluation by honest means and by presenting his or her client's case in a straightforward and clear manner.

(f) An advocate's strategy is to assist the adjudicator to appreciate, by sustainable agreements, that it would be proper, lawful, fair and equitable to make a finding in favour of his or her client;

(g) In a non-adjudicatory ADR it is for an advocate to provide the neutral adviser with necessary details and information in addition to identifying the contentions;

(h) The advocate and the opposition side should not however feel threatened; he or she must also be able to present his or her client's case in a cogent manner on the basis of understanding of the issues, and why the neutral adviser should find in his/her favour. In other words, advocates on both sides should be extremely conversant with each party's case. In fact, having understood each party's strengths and weaknesses, the advocates should initiate negotiations even before being involved in a non-adjudicatory process;

(i) Finally, an advocate must be honest with himself or herself that he/she understood the objectives of ADR, and whether he/she may be able to do justice to the parties and the tribunal.

Brown and Marriott suggested that the following practical observations might be helpful in identifying an advocate's function in a non-adjudicatory process:

(a) Contrary to the popular belief, an advocate's personal style and demeanour in court proceedings or in ADR is of minor relevance to the outcome; neutral advisers are concerned with issues of rights and duties of parties, and therefore a belligerent approach to support the client's case would be highly counter-productive.

(b) A convincing submission is useful for various reasons – it represents the understanding of the facts of the advocate concerned, it should contain a balanced view of each party's case, and it should clearly identify the reasons why he or she would like to have a friendly settlement through a non-adjudicatory ADR.

(c) In making his or her submissions, references to documentary evidence, including diagrams, tables etc may be made by an advocate; in fact, in many instances submission of cases by such technical methods proved to be very useful.

(d) A good advocate would be particular about the time limits agreed between the parties or stipulated by the neutral advisers. It is very important that presentation and submission of case are not unnecessarily elaborate whereby a non-adjudicatory process would be worse than court proceedings[2].

An advocate should have expertise in communicating and negotiating; this becomes even more important when the parties are of foreign origins and unfamiliar with the English system. Communication skill is essential in concluding any successful negotiation. It is, therefore, also essential that a good advocate is neutral and understands the cultural backgrounds of the parties. These issues have received attention in a separate section of this work.

A good advocate's function would be to familiarise parties with the system and the probable remedies he or she may have. This is a special quality that cannot be taught by any means, it has to be learnt by an advocate. If, however, the parties speak foreign languages then the settlement process becomes difficult, but it is the advocate's and the neutral's function to ensure that the parties' position is not jeopardised for that reason; hence the need for learning

[2] On these points see Henry Brown and Arthur Marriott, op. cit., at pp 303–304

the skills of communication and negotiation. There must not be any "take it or leave it" approach in the alternative dispute resolution approach[3].

One of the most important considerations must be to clarify the position of the parties and the situation in which they find themselves, as well as the nature of remedies that may be offered to them. Furthermore, the consequences of entering into litigation or court proceedings must also be clearly identified. In other words, an advocate must be honest, straightforward, conversant with the legal system and must be able to present the case to his or her party first identifying the strengths and weaknesses and the strategies that he or she would like to adopt in settling the dispute[4].

Informal confidential meetings between the parties and the mediator may provide good opportunities for settling disputes on the basis of new reflections on the issues but always bearing in mind that a mediator, who is in reality a communicator, must not impose his ideas on the parties.

Where lawyers may participate as representatives of parties, they should by training adopt an attitude which is not belligerent, oppressive or adversarial. The willingness to settle disputes by amicable means after clearly identifying the nature of the issues and the legal consequences is a primary function of the lawyers in such situations.

A lawyer should behave himself or herself in such a way that parties must be prepared to accept him or her as a conciliator so that they can be more frank with a third party, and it is for the lawyer to win the confidence of the parties so as to facilitate the conciliation process.

In order to make a non-adjudicatory ADR a success, it is essential that people taking the initiative in such a system should prepare alternative strategies to settle the dispute if the first strategy should fail.

Alternative strategies may be developed only if the mediator and the lawyer or any third party have a thorough understanding of the case. It is natural that parties will initially remain adamant about their own respective positions and hence there is the need to explain the parties' position in clear terms with alternative strategies with no coercive attempts being made to settle the dispute.

6.4 TRAINING OF NEUTRAL ADVISERS

Without proper training a neutral adviser may not render the services which are expected of him. Although a uniform set of training may be devised for neutral advisors, it must be borne in mind that settlers of disputes in England come from a wide range of background including barristers, solicitors, engineers, architects, quantity surveyors, academics and even community workers; therefore the regulation of people from a variety of disciplines presents a

[3] Henry Brown and Arthur Marriott, op. cit., at p 305

[4] See further Henry Brown and Arthur Marriott, op. cit., at p 306

difficulty although they must be subject to a code of conduct whether binding or voluntary.

There does not exist any particular criterion for selecting neutral advisors although in selecting them attention should be paid to the nature of the dispute and the particular expertise of the adviser. It is essential to consolidate the selection criteria, although too rigid criteria would defeat the purpose. Furthermore, parties have freedom to choose their own neutral advisors.

Whereas the Centre for Effective Dispute Resolution (CEDR) does not seem to have a definite criteria for the appointment of mediators, it draws neutral advisors from professional and/or business backgrounds. The Family Mediators Association requires a prospective mediator either to be an experienced family lawyer or a person who possesses qualifications and experience in social work, psychiatry, counselling, conciliation etc. The National Association of Family Associations and Conciliation Services has established their selection criteria based on educational and professional qualifications; on the other hand, local community mediation schemes do not generally require any professional or educational prerequisites.

Whether or not an institution establishes any selection criteria in the interests of justice and fairness to the parties, it would only be fair to appoint advisors and mediators whose suitability, both professionally and academically, for conducting mini trials or actual dispute settlement may not be questioned. There is no doubt that a degree of quality control must be maintained in order to ensure that parties have confidence in the person and the institution concerned. Where a dispute involves consideration of legal issues, appointment of an advisor or a mediator should be based on the legal experience of an advisor or a mediator or a negotiator in addition to other requirements. In general, however, training schemes are available for people who wish to be qualified mediators, and in England, amongst other institutions, CEDR, the British Academy of Experts, Mediation UK, the Family Mediators Association, the National Association of Family Mediation and Conciliation Services, offer training to interested people. In 1992, the Law Society's Second Report on alternative dispute resolution recognised alternative dispute resolution as a priority area of training for solicitors in order to allow them to represent their clients in mediation and also for coming to the aid of their clients. Although there is a need for a formal training for settling disputes in the alternative dispute resolution system, the fact remains that such training may have its own limits as, in the final analysis, the understanding of the person of the purpose of alternative dispute resolution, his ability to become a negotiator and his friendly attitude to settling a dispute after comprehending the nature of the issues matter most[5]. What is to be emphasised is that a lawyer's approach to settling disputes within a fixed courtroom framework must be avoided, as must the creation of a court environment.

[5] In this connection one may like to refer to the opinion of Simon Roberts in his article entitled "Mediation and Family Disputes", *Modern Law Review*, 1983 at 555

It must be pointed out that the training of neutral advisers should centre around the issue of how to develop a sense of neutrality and maintain it throughout the ADR process; in other words, a neutral adviser must not proceed from a position of bias or any perceived ideas about the parties or their case. Having comprehended the case, he/she must advise the parties as to the nature of the issues and how best they may be settled. He/she must strike a proper balance so that no party is adversely affected by his/her advice.

A neutral adviser should not accept the position unless he/she has thorough competence in the subject matter of the dispute, be it related to consumer protection, family, construction or other issues.

Where parties may be of foreign origin, like representatives, neutral advisers should ensure that they are clear about the ADR procedure in England, and the matters in dispute. Thus, like representatives, neutral advisers, must also be tolerant and clear in their statements.

6.5 FUNDING OF ADR

Although the ADR system of settling disputes should, in principle, be less expensive than court proceedings or arbitral proceedings, certain expenses are nevertheless inevitable in the system. This section discusses the possible sources of funding for parties choosing to have their disputes settled through the ADR system.

Usually, no legal aid is made available for alternative dispute resolution whether the dispute is of a civil, commercial or family nature. In other words, the alternative dispute resolution system effectively relies on private funding; hence the need for keeping the cost to a minimum, particularly when the parties are without sufficient financial means.

In commercial and civil alternative dispute resolutions, costs are equally shared between the parties; therefore costs must be agreed upon at the beginning. The Law Society's Report on Alternative Dispute Resolution, 1991, pointed out that legal aid should be made available to alternative dispute resolution at least in selected types of cases. Its Second Report on Alternative Dispute Resolution published in 1992, stated that:

> *"Of course, ACAS offers the services of its officials in order to assist employers and employees in resolving their disputes through its conciliation services. In certain cases district judges offer to help the parties to negotiate their disputes, mostly in matrimonial matters."*

Unless state funds are made available, either in the form of legal aid or in any other form from the Department of Constitutional Affairs, the progress of alternative dispute resolution might be hindered. Of course, various insurance companies cover legal expenses but not those incurred for alternative dispute resolution.

6.6 CONCLUSIONS

This chapter explains the basic criteria that must be satisfied in a non-adjudicatory ADR and the nature of training neutral advisers should have. The fundamental issues are simple and in that no judicial features should become manifest in the process. The third party and the advocate's function would be to settle the dispute by friendly means. The purpose is not to reach a settlement by coercive means but to make clear why a friendly settlement is preferable to a settlement by judicial process. But this may not be achieved unless the strategies have been correctly identified and alternative strategies have been thought of and offered. Such strategies can only be made and offered when a thorough understanding of each party's case can be assumed. In a non-adjudicatory ADR an adviser's role would mainly be that of negotiator, and in negotiating the differences he or she must understand the nature of relief and remedies to which each party is entitled.

Once a negotiation has been satisfactorily reached it must be formalised by drafting the negotiated settlement. The drafting must be in a simple form in order to ensure that it is clear to both parties; it must be free of jargon and drafted in unambiguous terms. It must be shown to both parties to ensure that they have understood the terms on which the settlement has been reached and what may be required of each party to implement the settlement. One of the questions that must be made clear is whether the terms of a negotiated settlement are binding. In order to make a settlement binding, an order of the court would be necessary and therefore the governing law should be identified in the settlement agreement.

Problems may arise however if proceedings are pending in court; in that event the parties must agree that court proceedings on the same issues must be kept in abeyance and that the legal costs must be distributed in an amicable fashion. Provisions should also be made to say what action might be taken if the negotiated settlement is not to be acted upon, that is, whether the matter should be referred to an arbitral tribunal or a court. If the negotiated settlement is to remain confidential, a statement to that effect must be made, and where certain matters must be allowed to continue, such as the welfare of a child, the conditions of such welfare issues must be detailed. In other words, depending upon the nature of a dispute, the settlement must provide for special circumstances.

The negotiated settlement must be signed by both parties and it must be confirmed by the parties personally or through their representatives.

As to the training of neutral advisers, it has been stated that it is of utmost importance that advisers learn how to remain neutral and, indeed, maintain their neutrality throughout an ADR process. Furthermore, neutral advisers must be certain themselves that they are able to guide the parties through their skills and expertise.

CHAPTER 7

Mediation in Progress

7.1 INTRODUCTION

In this chapter an attempt is made to illustrate how the mediation process should be actually activated and what would be each party's role in the mediation process. In developing this chapter attention is paid to the psychological factors that often seem to influence a mediation process and also the formalities that a mediator, in particular, is required to complete. It is maintained however that the mediation process can be different in respect of different types of dispute, but this chapter attempts to identify the common elements that become evident in a mediation process.

7.2 HOW TO INITIATE MEDIATION

Initiation of mediation is the most difficult task to achieve as at this stage the relationship between the parties is not only acrimonious but also one of *"never to meet again."* At this stage even a third party's intervention to initiate a friendly settlement proves to be difficult; nevertheless a neutral third party may be required to put forward suggestions to the other side without giving the impression that the party on whose initiative mediation is intended to be initiated has some weakness. The idea is to point out that an unresolved dispute should not be kept in that state for an indefinite period of time. In the process of persuading parties, no specific formula can be applied; depending upon the circumstances of each case and the attitude of parties towards the settlement, the nature of their grievances and the kind of remedies that may be offered, a suggestion to ADR may be put forward. Of course, if a contract contains a clause whereby ADR may be used for settling any dispute arising under that contract then it is important to activate that clause.

The legal issue remains that, in the event of a party refusing to participate in ADR for settling its disputes, a breach of contractual obligation would not arise. If an ADR clause has been incorporated into a contract for settling their disputes under that contract then it becomes a binding obligation on the parties.

In the United Kingdom there is no obligation however for anybody to accept ADR mandatorily, although courts in England and Wales seem to be encouraging the use of ADR. Under the High Court Practice Direction lawyers are required to indicate whether or not ADR has been discussed but no more than that. In other words, ADR in the United Kingdom is, in most cases, a voluntary affair. This is not to suggest that this is a time-wasting effort but only to point out that there is no obligation to use it mandatorily. Where there is no contractual or court-related ADR the only alternative left for settling disputes under a non-court procedure would be persuasion and for a successful persuasion considerable skill and tactics are necessary.

The persuasion process can take place in four different ways:

(a) Party to party – which initially becomes extremely difficult if one party without any notion to surrender to the other party takes the initiative to suggest a settlement by an ADR method, but eventually, it might work.

(b) Lawyer to lawyer contact often becomes heavy-handed although they should be able to identify the issues and problems in a very articulate fashion; it should also be their duty to point out the comparative advantages and disadvantages of the ADR process and court proceedings.

(c) The officers of third parties may actually prove successful in persuading the parties to mediate a dispute. One of the recent examples of good offices as a matter of persuading parties to mediate was a dispute between Eurotunnel and TML over claims pertaining to the construction of the Channel Tunnel. Pressure from the governments of France and the United Kingdom and shareholders was brought to bear upon the parties to negotiate their dispute which they failed to do[1].

(d) Finally, a party has a prerogative to approach an ADR organisation.

Whatever approach may be taken and whatever third party may be involved in using ADR as the dispute settlement system, it must fully clarify to the parties what is involved in the system and in what way or ways ADR may be better than court proceedings. Parties' non-coercive consent is essential to activating ADR as a dispute settlement method.

7.3 PARTICIPANTS IN MEDIATION

Participants in this context should be categorised into two categories:

(a) the parties to a dispute, and

(b) the mediator(s).

The main participants are obviously the parties to a dispute, the mediator would simply take the role of a referee with the duty to put the parties onto the right track having explained to them the real issues in the dispute. A mediator

[1] K Mackie, D Miles, W Marsh, op. cit., at 84

is not a participant *stricto sensu* although he will be involved in the dispute settlement, but he must remain neutral.

Mediation is an interactive dispute settlement process; and this process admits of formalities and informalities. Whereas the parties to a dispute are required to be active in interacting between themselves, the function of the mediator is to control the conduct of that interactive process and try to ensure that an amicable result is reached. Whereas in the event of a successful mediation, parties benefit, no benefit accrues to a mediator. Thus, a mediator is a special type of participant in a mediation process.

In this chapter an attempt is made to examine the role of participants in a mediation process including that of an expert witness and legal representatives, and how a mediation progresses.

7.3.1 The Parties

Parties as participants in a mediation process are not supposed to be trained people; in fact, they are parties with grievances; therefore, an articulate presentation or conduct may not necessarily be expected of them although, in general, they are often well-composed and well-prepared with their cases. It is for the mediator to explain to them the nature of their function and participation and the purpose of agreeing to come to a mediation process. Although they are expected to show their willingness to negotiate their claims, often it befalls the mediator to create that willingness in the minds of the parties. In other words, the parties may arrive at a mediation process without a total commitment.

During preliminary conferences a mediator is required to explain to the parties the merits and weaknesses in the mediation process in order to allow them to compare it with those of court proceedings. Furthermore, a mediator should also explain to them that without their commitment to reaching a negotiated settlement mediation may not succeed. The parties are therefore required to be informed of the need for an inter-active role, total disclosure of facts and issues, and, when necessary, the need for maintaining confidentiality.

On the other hand, it is no harm for a party to inform himself or herself beforehand of what is required of him or her at a mediation. It is not necessary for a party to use technical jargon nor is it necessary for it to be mindful of formalities, but after the agenda has been developed, the parties should go through the mediation process in accordance with the agenda although there is no need to maintain the rigid application of an agenda. A party should not be concerned with its bargaining power. In the proper sense of the term, bargaining power in reality stands for power to negotiate. Communication skills and full knowledge of the issues are the most important requirements for a productive participation by a party in a mediation process. A party is also required to appreciate that the other side may also have certain genuine issues and claims. Parties must be conscious of the importance of utilising time and the need to narrow down the issues of differences between themselves. The more a mediation process is prolonged unnecessarily the more remote is the prospect of its success. Parties must be responsible and must have the commitment to reach an amicable settlement and to be prepared to consider the other side's claims and issues too. It is important that the parties themselves do not frustrate the purposes of the mediation.

7.3.2 Legal Representatives

Where a dispute is already in litigation or involves large claims or entails complex legal issues the parties may engage solicitors and barristers for their participation in the mediation process. In such a situation the mediation becomes a law-orientated one and may be similar to court proceedings. Furthermore, the parties' role may be subordinated by their lawyers' role and the lawyers might express their ideas in complex legal jargon which would be beyond the comprehension of the parties. This is not to suggest that lawyers should not participate on behalf of their clients but perhaps legally qualified mediator(s) would be preferable in such cases as they are fully aware of their functions as mediators as well as the legal implications of various claims that may be put forward by the parties. In fact, where legal representation is allowed, a mediator is often required to remind them of their remit in order to ensure that a forum suitable for court proceedings is not allowed to be created. There is no reason why even in the presence of legal representatives the parties cannot make their own opening statements, but the parties should always be provided with an opportunity to supplement these statements in their own words, if necessary. It might be appropriate to allow legal representatives to make the final submissions on behalf of their clients. In cases related to personal injuries or disputes relating to construction or engineering contracts, participation of legal representatives might prove to be helpful for the mediator to identify the bases for claiming damages and their calculation[2].

Again, perhaps the best method is to allow the parties to interact between themselves and during breaks they should obtain advice from their legal representative and continue with the mediation process by drawing the attention of the mediator to the ideas they have gained from their legal representatives. Settlement of disputes by mediation is different from that by court proceedings; it is therefore essential, where possible, to limit participation of legal representatives and maintain the interactive role of the parties. It is essential for the mediator to determine at what point legal representatives might be allowed to make their representations.

[2] In practice, however, in determining the basis for damages and computing the damages assistance from Quantity Surveyor and/or Engineer on the case will usually be sought.

7.3.3 Experts

In respect of technical issues, an expert's opinion may be necessary. Experts are usually appointed with the consent of the parties involved in a dispute. An expert is required to prepare and submit his/her report to the legal representatives by the stipulated date. Each party will have the right to appoint its expert. The common elements in these reports will, of course, determine the nature of the technical issues and the probable causal-link of the issues. Expert opinions are sought only for clarification of issues; they do not form part of any decision. Experts must be neutral.

7.3.4 Mediator(s)

To mediate means to intervene between disputants to settle a dispute. Thus, a mediator is a person whose function is to settle a dispute between disputants. But what kind of person should be a mediator? A mediator intervenes because the disputants have allowed him to do so. In this sense, *"intervention"* is not the most appropriate word. A mediator is invited by the parties to provide advice as to how to settle their dispute.

A mediator is a person who must have a thorough understanding of the dispute from historical, societal, political, economic and legal points of view. He/she must have no bias for or against any party. Having understood the primary and secondary causes of a dispute, he/she is required to understand the legal issues involved in order to make the parties to a dispute aware of their respective legal position.

A mediator is a person who has already established his/her reputation as a person who possesses knowledge in international affairs, and has demonstrated his/her knowledge in particular disputes.

Unlike a conciliator, a mediator advises the parties what they should do, advice which may not be accepted by parties; thus a mediation effort may fail. This may be evidenced by the failure of mediation in the cases of Northern Ireland and Camp David (Arab-Israeli conflict).

In the context of this Chapter it is necessary to explain how and in what circumstances these qualities may be utilised by an ideal mediator. A mediator must build trust and confidence in the minds of the parties by demonstrating his knowledge of the facts of the case and the issues involved in it. He must remain neutral and he must explain his position to the parties in conducting mediation and emphasise that it is for the parties to take an active role in reaching a settlement. He must also explain to the parties their responsibilities in making honest and truthful statements, full disclosure of issues and facts, remaining calm and appreciating each party's claim and grievances. In order to assure the parties of his neutrality and impartiality, he should emphasise whether he is governed by any code of conduct or whether it would be possible for the parties to bring any allegations against him. Departure from impartiality and neutrality will necessarily jeopardise a mediation process and therefore the parties should be encouraged by the mediator to express their feelings at any stage whether the mediator departed from these essential criteria. The mediator must also implement the rules of natural justice.

7.4 THE OPENING PHASE

The opening of a mediation process may prove to be difficult in that unless a mediator can build confidence in the minds of the parties and is able to offer his services in a friendly fashion, the mediator and the mediation process might not succeed. It is therefore essential that at the initial stage a mediator puts the parties' mind at ease and creates a friendly environment and yet remains courteous and professional. This is where the experience of a mediator becomes relevant. He or she must not show any bias towards or against anybody. He/she must build confidence in the parties' mind by demonstrating that he/she has already understood the basic issues in the dispute.

Every mediation is unique in that the structure of mediation must be developed according to the nature of the dispute and the needs of the parties. It is primarily a party-based activity which is the most important distinguishing factor between mediation and arbitration and court procedure.

Mediation can be used at any stage of a dispute even when a dispute is already subject to litigation. This is perhaps the most important characteristic and type of contribution that mediation can make to the realm of dispute settlement. It does not generally admit of a strict procedure although ideally it should progress in accordance with an agenda. Where however mediation is institutional it must follow the rule of that institution.

The mediator must also make a statement detailing the purposes of the meeting and the role that each party is required to take. However, in no way should the mediator intimidate the parties. In explaining issues a mediator must use simple language so that no confusion is created in the mind of any of the parties. Furthermore, he must assure the parties of their right to seek clarification on any of the issues concerned. One of the most important duties of a mediator at this stage is to create an environment of informality whereby the parties may feel at ease to ask questions and for clarification, although the mediator might suggest that questions might also be raised after the end of a particular phase of the process. If a mediator should wish to follow a particular procedure, these must be clearly explained to the parties and their representatives but he or she must ensure that no complex rules of procedure overtake the atmosphere of informality.

A mediator usually makes an opening statement, which should not be too long in order to explain to the parties the purpose of coming to the mediation, the differences between mediation and court proceedings and what would be the end result of mediation if it succeeds. At this stage a confident mediator should explain his own position, his duty to ethics and an assurance of neutrality. It is important that at this stage the mediator emphasises the importance of informality and co-operation between the parties and the importance of submitting the documents and evidence as precisely as possible rather than making it a forum for altercation. The mediator must also assure the parties that he or she will not fail to observe the rules of natural justice.

If, however, during a mediation process the environment turns out to be unfriendly, a competent mediator should know how to deal with this situation, and in particular, by allowing what is known as *"a cooling off period"*. The success or failure of a mediation very much depends upon how a mediator conducts a mediation and how much confidence he or she has built in the minds of the parties to make their opening statements and the basic issues of these statements.

7.5 PARTIES' OPENING STATEMENTS

As the title of this section suggests, at this stage, it is for the parties to submit their statements whether by themselves or by their legal representatives. But ideally, these statements should be allowed to be made by the parties themselves as the parties know their cases best. If statements are made by the parties themselves, it is natural, that sometimes inarticulate expressions may be made by the parties and the mediator should appreciate that or seek clarification of meanings, if necessary. The parties are required to make factual statements rather than making references to the law. Where however parties insist on presenting their statements through their legal representatives a mediator is required to respect their request and ensure that whatever a legal representative might submit is understood by the parties themselves.

At all stages a mediator must ensure that from a psychological standpoint both parties are fully satisfied as to the way he or she is conducting the mediation. Where a matter requires an expert opinion in advance, the mediator may ask the expert(s) a few questions for the purpose of clarifying certain issues.

It is for the party who initiates the mediation to make the first statement, although no hard and fast rule about it needs to be followed it is the most logical thing to do. In making their statements, the parties should identify the main issues clearly in respect of each other's position and it must be assumed that the mediator is already familiar with basic issues. However, the parties or their legal representatives should be allowed to make a brief statement of their respective cases in order to allow the parties opportunities to contest the factual aspects of the case, if necessary. One advantage of allowing the parties or their legal representative to submit their statements is that through the process of making these statements the mediator can also verify his or her own understanding of the case.

One of the important objectives of allowing the parties to make their respective statements is to ensure that he or she is able to identify the real contention in the dispute and communictae this to the parties. If anybody's understanding of the issues is to be corrected it must be done so at that stage. Opening statements are not meant to bring out controversies but to identify each other's issues.

7.6 AGENDA SETTING

From an organisational point of view it is always preferable to set an agenda for proceeding with mediation. This is even more important for the sake of the parties who should be informed in advance of the order of issues/topics that a mediator is going to follow. The aim of agenda-setting is to list topics for the entire course of mediation and in what order they will be dealt with. Obviously, an effective agenda may not be set unless the issues have been clearly identified and agreed by both parties and the mediator. It should be pointed out however that no rigidity should be maintained about following the agenda; a mediator should be prepared to re-organise the agenda or amend it with the consent of the parties.

It is not obligatory to set an agenda to carry out a mediation but nevertheless it provides a structure which would help the parties to consolidate the arguments in a constructive fashion. Another advantage of setting an agenda is to confirm the issues to which both parties have consented. An agenda thus provides a ground work for mediation. In setting an agenda a progression of items should be maintained, for example, first clarification of mutually agreed items, then clarification of differences of the parties and thereafter the possible way forward, and finally the remedial measures that may be available to the affected party.

It must be emphasised that the compensation aspect of a case should not be discussed first; instead the liabilities of the parties should be determined first. In this respect, a mediation process may like to follow the pattern of court proceedings, especially in arranging issues in order. Once an agreed agenda has been developed, the mediation should proceed in accordance with the agenda although, as stated earlier, a degree of flexibility must be allowed in changing the agenda, if necessary.

7.7 THE SESSIONS

During the first session the parties start communicating directly with each other rather than going through the mediator. A mediator simply works as a referee at this stage to ensure that the parties are on track and try to settle the issues. Direct communications between the parties has the advantage of breaking the ice and creating as amicable a solution as possible. Thus, during the discussion, if the parties disagree too much or become disruptive it is for the mediator to put them back on track and allow them to carry on with their interaction. The purpose of the initial session is to get to know the parties and familiarise the mediator with the facts and issues. During the first session emotional outbursts often take place and a mediator may like to allow them within limits with a view to informing himself or herself of the demands and needs of the parties. Where however the parties fail to communicate to each other truly and frankly, the mediator should encourage them to interact on specific issues, both in the interests of the parties and the mediator himself or herself.

At this session the mediator would require the parties to follow the agenda items in order to explore issues for themselves. This exercise is extremely important for identification by the mediator of the extent of understanding or misunderstanding of the issues by the parties and whether they are prepared to negotiate. The first session is also extremely important for ascertaining the underlying conflicts of issues between the parties. In fact, it becomes a learning session for the mediator and the parties. Another function of the mediator at this session is to help the parties in putting their points out clearly according to their individual perceptions so that at a later stage the mediator can clarify the bases for misunderstanding of the issues by the parties. The presence of the mediator at this session proves to be extremely useful in that the parties generally feel the need to become as effective as possible in their discussions. The discussions between the parties at this stage might also give rise to real issues which the mediator should take into account and amend the agenda accordingly, if necessary.

During the initial session the mediator should allow the parties to be engaged in *"free play"* but they must not digress too much from the main track. The mediator must be careful; he or she must not intervene unduly and lose thereby confidence and respect. Where a bottleneck situation may take place, the mediator may gently intervene to deal with the situation by emphasising the areas of agreement between the parties and the importance of carrying on with the discourse. Of course, a mediator can seek clarification of issues from the parties during the initial discussion. In conducting the first session, in particular, a mediator should also understand that the parties may unduly delve into emotional aspects of the issues, and tolerate this to a certain extent, instead of restraining the expression of feelings. The initial session therefore is crucial in nature in many respects; it helps both the parties and the mediator in understanding the nature of the issues and the differences between the parties. Before the initial session is ended a mediator must ensure that all relevant issues have been identified and discussed by the parties.

7.7.1 Private Sessions of the Parties

When the initial session reaches its final stage it would be useful for a mediator to summarise in an unbiased fashion the discussions of the parties and to see whether the parties agree to that summary. If the parties so agree, the mediator then should proceed with private sessions of the parties and allocate equal time to each party. At the beginning of each private session the mediator should remind the party of the need for maintaining confidentiality of information so that they are regarded as privileged information. It is clear that there is no need to hold a private session unless the first session has proved to be effective; in other words, the first session should provide the ground for private sessions with the parties. It is quite possible however to go straight into the negotiating stage if the areas of disagreement appear to be minimal.

At a private session, a mediator should be able to learn more about the underlying causes of the dispute if those causes have not been sufficiently revealed in the initial session. A private session would prove to be meaningless if the parties do not feel safe to disclose to the mediator information of a confidential nature. At private sessions a mediator may thus learn new information which is vitally important for his understanding of the case. It is therefore important that the mediator assures the parties that he will not disclose any information of a confidential nature to the other party. It needs to be emphasised at this stage that the parties will feel safe to disclose information to the mediator if he or she has behaved himself or herself in such a way as to develop the required degree of confidence in him or her.

Neutrality of the mediator is particularly important in that knowledge of confidential information must not develop any bias in him or her. At the private session a mediator should be extremely attentive to any information which is of a confidential nature. He or she can, of course, seek clarification of such information from the party concerned.

Ideally, a mediator should hold the first private session with the claimant although in general no rigid policy is maintained on this issue. In holding private session with the parties, a mediator must remain absolutely neutral in order to ensure that no party may have an iota of suspicion about his objectivity and ask questions only for the purposes of clarifying issues in his or her mind. In fact, one of the primary purposes of holding private sessions with parties is to build rapport with them so that they feel the mediator is the most appropriate person to help them out. What kinds of question should be raised in private session depends on the nature of a dispute and a mediator may ascertain what kind of solution the party may wish to reach. At such sessions, a mediator may also try to ascertain the connection between cause and effect and ask the parties to explain every single detail of the incident. During private sessions it is often possible for a mediator to think of new settlement options and test the reaction of parties to these options. Private sessions are meant for specific purposes; therefore they should seek answers to specific questions and should not entail lengthy discussions. Parties should be asked to justify the demands including the basis for calculation of damages or compensation as the case may be. It would be advisable for a mediator to identify the weaknesses of a party in respect of its case.

7.7.2 Joint Session for Negotiation

Joint sessions for negotiation can be held immediately after the initial stage is over with clear clarification of issues and after conclusions of private sessions. At the beginning of the negotiation stage a mediator should once again summarise to the parties the areas of agreement and disagreement and the possible consequences particularly in respect of costs of referring the matters of disagreement to a court of law. He should emphasise these issues in clear terms at the beginning of the negotiation session. It is to be stressed however that this session should not be unduly overburdened with legal issues and no attempt should be made to establish one's own bargaining position. In this respect lawyers should appreciate the reasons for referring the matter to mediation and take particular care to ensure that a mediation session is not transformed into a session of court proceedings. A fixed position by any party must be discouraged by a mediator and he or she should direct a negotiation session to a conclusion after reminding the parties of their respective strengths and weaknesses. At this stage a mediator should also provide all the options for settlement reminding the parties of the underlying causes of their differences. If at the negotiation stage no settlement is initially reached the parties should be allowed opportunities by the mediator to reflect on their respective positions without imposing on the parties his or her own choices. The parties must reach their settlement on mutually agreed terms, and any coercion to agree to terms by a mediator must be avoided.

7.7.3 The Final Stage

The purpose of this stage is to achieve a final agreement on all the issues, confirming that the dispute between the parties has come to an end. It is very much for the mediator to take control of this stage. He should summarise the issues on which the parties have already reached agreement, and encourage the parties to resolve their differences in respect of the other issues, so that the parties take a more pro-active role in settling their differences. The mediator should also ensure that the agreed solution of the dispute is finally accepted by the parties concerned. It is thus clear that the nature of the progress to be made at this stage very much depends upon what has been achieved in the first and second stages of discussion and understanding of the issues by the parties.

If the parties agree to the nature of their dispute, they should be asked to draft their terms of settlement; the mediator should not intervene at this stage as he/she has already explained to the parties what would be the best terms of agreement. If the parties are represented by lawyers, then the latter usually draft the terms of the agreement; however, caution should be taken in drafting terms of the agreement in simple language, which would not give rise to any controversy, particularly as regards interpretation of particular terms or words.

The mediator should however be present to offer his/her help in drafting the terms of the agreement. The agreed terms of the agreement must be signed by both parties.

7.8 THE MEDIATOR'S UNDERSTANDING OF THE NATURE OF THE DISPUTE

A mediator is required to understand the internal dynamics of the dispute, that is, the reasons for the underlying conflicts between the parties. By studying the case, a mediator should have a basic idea of the underlying conflicts between the parties. A competent mediator should tactfully explain this to the parties in a very courteous and friendly fashion. In fact, a clear expression of the conflicts may develop confidence in the mediator in the minds of the parties.

A mediator must be extremely attentive to the words used by the parties or their legal representatives in making their statements; they may also reveal the parties' underlying conflicts. He/she should make a note of the crucial statements made by the parties or their legal representatives in order to understand the need of the parties. This is where the basic difference between court proceedings and mediation lies. A court goes by the law. A mediator must ascertain what each party wants, and each party's reaction to the other party's issues. He/she must clarify the bases for differences between the parties. This process is known as the dynamics of the dispute.

A mediator must also understand why the differences in the parties arose – the emotional aspects and misunderstanding of issues on the part of each party. In other words, a mediator is required to look behind the events described and the lack of communication, if any, between the parties, which might have contributed to the misunderstanding. A mediator's primary duty is not to look for the law, but to see the reasons for the misunderstanding between the parties which caused the dispute.

An important strategy in a mediation process is to diffuse hostility by understanding the reasons for the hostility. A mediator must know how to diffuse hostility, and have the capability of transforming a negative situation into a positive one, that is, change a situation of hostility to that of friendliness. A mediator should bank on the positive statements that parties have made, formally or informally, and try to convince the parties that the areas of difference between them are minimal; or alternatively, if they are not minimal, they should be identified as such, and the parties should be asked to try to reach an amicable solution of the differences between them. It is, of course, for a mediator to help reach an amicable solution by identifying the misunderstanding between them as to the terms of a contract or of an issue, and the consequences of instituting legal proceedings in an attempt to resolve their misunderstanding and differences.

After the opening statements made by the parties, a mediator should make a summary of each of the statements, and identify the issues before negotiations take place by using, where necessary, some of the actual expressions used by the parties. The parties may also be asked by the mediator to supplement any issue, if necessary. At this point, a mediator should identify the areas for agreement and disagreement between the parties. The psychology of this process is that a party may not pay much attention to what the other party is stating, but they may pay much attention to what a mediator says about his/her understanding of the dispute.

7.9 NEGATIVES

Attempts at mediation might fail. This section identifies the symptoms and outcome of failure to mediate; these have been described as *"negatives"*, which in this context stands for the hindrances in successfully concluding a deal. A number of situations may come under this, but the primary ones are:

7.9.1 Threatened Walk Out

A threatened walk out becomes apparent when a party still maintains that it has a very strong case and that there is no need to mediate or negotiate, even though its perception as to its stronger position may not be well-founded. In such a situation, the mediator should in a private session, try to convince the party concerned to appreciate the reality of his case.

But, of course, if the party does have a stronger position, and he would like to have his remedies through court proceedings, a mediator may not be able to prevent him from instituting court proceedings.

7.9.2 Lack of Communication between the Parties

This is a very unfortunate situation, but it may occur. The mediator after private session should realise that there would be little point in proceeding with the mediation process. Incidentally, here is an issue on which a mediator should reflect, whether any particular circumstances were responsible for not breaking the communication barrier between the parties.

7.9.3 Lack of Confidence / Faith in Mediation

The introductory session with the mediator is supposed to deal with the merits and weaknesses of mediation; it is maintained, however, despite all efforts made by a mediator, a party may still remain unconvinced about the effectiveness of mediation. It is a matter of perception, which is largely responsible for the lack of confidence or faith in mediation.

7.10 CONCLUSIONS

There are two primary issues on which the success of a mediation depends: (a) the nature of the dispute; and (b) the conduct of the mediation process of a mediator. Where a dispute is predominantly concerned with complex legal issues, such as in shipping cases, it may not be very suitable for mediation; furthermore, immediate enforcement of decisions becomes an issue in such cases; otherwise, there is no reason why commercial cases or even construction and engineering disputes may not be resolved by a mediation process. A mediator must not only effectively mediate, but also make mediation an alternative not by promoting it as a dispute settlement process but by developing commitment of the parties to it.

The stages explained in this chapter are crucial to the success of mediation. During these stages, alternative strategies for settlement should be developed, as the mediation process progresses or regresses. Parties should be advised during the initial stages of a mediation process to bring out their grievances in order to allow their mediator(s) to appreciate the underlying conflict, if any, between the parties. Often written alternatives, as remedies, help for the parties to understand their respective position. As stated earlier, the primary purpose of holding a private session is to narrow down the areas of disagreement. A mediator should encourage parties, with justification, to abandon the claims which are not sustainable.

Where a mediation process breaks down, a mediator should prompt the parties to take a *"cooling off"* period. A mediation process may become a lengthy process giving rise to many unexpected situations. A mediator should be a quick-thinking person, full of ideas and patient. A mediator must be extremely familiar with the legal remedies available under recent statute(s) and inform the parties of them; and the amount of financial benefit to which a party may be entitled and the basis on which the amount is reached[3]. It is important to realise that if benefits and remedies out of a mediation do not match those that may be allowed by court proceedings, parties may not be persuaded to any mediation process.

In no circumstances shall a mediator give vent to anger or express his/her personal feelings about the dispute by any words or gestures. Whether fairness has been maintained by a mediator or not is confirmed by the parties; thus it is crucially important that a mediator does not take away the confidence which parties have placed in him.

A mediator must be able to *control* the mediation process. *"Control"* in this context would mean regulating the mediation process by discipline and reminding the parties of their duty to proceed with the mediation in accordance with the agenda. But in no event shall a mediator offend a party or give an impression of preferring one party to the other. To a certain extent, a mediator may be required to allow the parties, particularly during the initial stages, to let off steam, but always within limits. This is the time when a mediator may have to allow a *"cooling off"* period, or otherwise, a party may threaten to walk-out.

Undoubtedly, a mediator requires exemplary *communication skills*. He/she must be patient in order to understand the parties' cases, and must confirm that he/she has already understood them. This point is particularly important when the language of the mediator and that of the parties are not the same, but all of them nonetheless express themselves in an agreed common language. He/she shall ensure that every statement made by the parties is understood by him, including the body language, exposed by them.

A mediator must communicate in an unambiguous fashion and in a simple language. He must receive confirmation of this from the parties. He must not use any emotive expressions nor should he use any offensive words or any

[3] For a discussion of the issues involved in the stages of a mediation process, see further M. Noone, *Mediation*, Cavendish, London, (1996), Chapters 5 and 6

words which might be regarded as offensive by a party. This is especially important when mediation is sought by foreign parties.

Adaptability and flexibility – are two other important qualities which a mediator must possess and apply. As the interaction between the parties progresses, the mediator may have to adopt new strategies, bearing in mind that a decision-making process is predominantly by the parties for the parties; a mediator must not try to put the parties back on any pre-determined track. Flexibility in regard to time allocation to issues is also required to be maintained by a mediator.

A mediation process does not admit of any rigid procedure or standard of behaviour on the part of parties; it merely provides a framework for the resolution of a dispute. The concept of mediation requires a mediator to be adaptable to changed situations and flexible in accommodating the needs of the parties.

Mediation is primarily an interactive method of resolving disputes by the parties with minimal interaction by a mediator. He/she should not be an inquisitor, but nevertheless should raise questions for clarification of ideas in his/her mind. Where a mediator is required to raise questions he/she must not construct them in a way which would demonstrate his/her bias in favour or against any party. On the other hand, if during interaction, a particular issue raised by a party is not sufficiently clear to the other, a mediator may, with formal permission from the other side, clarify the issue. Enough questions are usually asked at private sessions; a mediator should restrain himself/herself from intervening unnecessarily at sessions at which parties interact. Questions should be of an open nature – *"tell me more about it"*, or *"how is that important for you"*; or *"what is really important for you"*. Again, open questions help clarify ideas, and parties may not feel hindered by such questions. By the same token, hypothetical questions may also be raised by a mediator; the purpose of raising such questions is to ascertain what the parties really would like to achieve. As stated earlier, a mediator is basically a referee that, on the basis of the performance of the parties, gives his verdict, but always in accordance with the law and the rules of natural justice.

The actual behaviour of the participants does not become evident until they are involved in the mediation process. The only predictable behaviour would be that of expert(s). But, then, this is a particular characteristic of a mediation process. A mediator's role in a mediation is extremely important in that he/she has the duty to encourage parties to take the initiative to reach a settlement. Where a party is rather introvert in nature or fails to become forthcoming, it is for the mediator to encourage it to actively participate in the process. The legal representative's role in a mediation process should be that of a legal saviour rather than pro-active. A mediator must ensure that a mediation process is not allowed to be a legal proceeding; thus the balance between legal discourse and fact-based discourse must be maintained; if a mediator is a lawyer, he/she should be able to strike this balance effectively at the appropriate point.

A mediator should not only be an amiable person, but also must possess the qualities of a case management expert, and an arbitrator. He must not only create a congenial environment for mediation but also maintain it throughout a mediation process, and the technique of achieving this has already been explained. Where, however, a mediator can, despite efforts, foresee that parties are very withdrawn and are inclined to prefer court proceedings, perhaps from an ethical point of view a mediator should not unduly prompt the parties to make further attempts at mediating their dispute. A mediator is required to be a patient listener, and an active resolver of disputes in a way which would protect the interest of both parties and offer them appropriate remedies.

The English judicial system is often criticised as being adversarial, giving the impression that an inquisitorial judicial system is preferable to an adversarial judicial system. There are advantages and disadvantages in both systems. Is an inquisitorial system much friendlier than an adversarial system? Is the court environment in an inquisitorial judicial system more user-friendly than that under an adversarial judicial system? Is an inquisitorial system necessarily less expensive than an adversarial system? Does not an adversarial judicial system entail the scope of amicable settlement which culminates in Tomlin orders? Does not an adversarial judicial system provide for settlement outside a court room? These are some of the questions which should be raised in considering the efficacy of the English judicial system. At the "pre-trial review" stage it often becomes clear whether to pursue court proceedings or whether to negotiate with the other party or parties.

Some authors[4] tend to give the impression that an adversarial judicial system is repugnant to mediation. Whether a dispute may be mediated or not largely depends upon the understanding of the issue by the lawyers (solicitors and barristers/advocates) involved in a course of action. In other words, it is to be considered whether the prospect of losing income under a mediation process may not prompt lawyers to resort to court proceedings. This is not to suggest that responsible lawyers divert cases into courts rather than mediation for a settlement, but only to point out that to date there exists no mechanism whereby lawyers would be required to go through a mediation process.

Furthermore, the perception of parties and lawyers as to the lack of enforceability of mediated decisions seems to be responsible for developing doubts as to the effectiveness of mediation as a mechanism for settling disputes.

What is to be considered seriously is whether the court proceedings are unduly over-criticised and the propriety of mediation is excessively justified. This is why the limits to a mediation process need to be rationally considered, and at the same time consider why an adversarial judicial system may not be entirely reformed to accommodate participatory dispute settlement procedure.

[4] See further K Mackie, D Miles, W Marsh, op. cit., and Brown and Marriott, op. cit.

Another issue that deserves consideration is whether mediation is a less expensive method of settling disputes than court proceedings, bearing in mind that when arbitration, as a method of settling disputes was popularised particularly during the 1970s and 1980s, it was soon found to be as expensive, if not more, as court proceedings. Furthermore, arbitration has already proved to be as complex a procedure as court proceedings.

There of course remains the rather insoluble issue as to what the legal status of mediators is: mediators are appointed by parties, but would parties be allowed to bring actions against mediators in negligence, if necessary? Is mediation going to be accepted as a compulsory part of judicial proceedings?

In order for more acceptability of mediation as a dispute settlement method, apparently the commercial world is required to change its attitude towards dispute settlement, recognising a shift from a stance of making attempts to a compulsory method of dispute settlement. If mediation becomes part of the judicial system, as a method of settling disputes, the provisions of the Human Rights Act 1998 will apply whereby these sessions may not be held in private. On the other hand, if the issue of privacy remains supreme in the case of mediations, it may never be part of the judicial system.

CHAPTER 8

Mini Trial

8.1 INTRODUCTION

Mini trial stands for a trial which would not culminate in a full trial and the purpose of which is to ascertain whether a dispute could be settled by what is known in England as the small claims or fast track method. In a mini trial, the parties effectively transform themselves into a tribunal and they are often assisted by a neutral expert. The lawyers present their respective clients' cases in a shorter version than usual. The presentation must be in accordance with the procedural rules agreed by the parties in advance. No determination is made at mini trials but the neutral expert might give a non-binding opinion in order to allow the parties to form their own views about their dispute. The primary purpose of such a trial is to short-circuit the process and make the parties aware of the nature of the issues and the legal implications and perhaps to convince them that a business or pragmatic judgment would be useful in settling their dispute. Through a mini trial a party should be able to visualise what might happen if the dispute had been referred to a full court hearing. The role of the neutral expert becomes crucial in mini trials; in the opinion of the Chartered Institute of Arbitrators it is a supervised settlement procedure. Another important purpose that a mini trial serves is to save money and time; it also prevents the parties from becoming involved in prolonged disagreements and controversy.

In this chapter an attempt is made to explain the basic procedures for holding mini trials.

8.2 PREPARATION

As the trial is short-circuited, in order for it to become effective it must be carefully planned. The organisations that conduct mini trials have their own procedures; nevertheless, it is possible to identify certain common procedures which are essential in the preparation of a mini trial:

(a) the venue and date(s) for the mini trial;

(b) the form of the mini trial, and

(c) the time-scale that may be allowed to conduct it.

This would mean that all other aspects of the trial, that is, discovery of documents, submissions, etc., have been completed before commencing the trial. In other words, the bundles must be comprehensive and must contain the essential documents. It must be determined beforehand how much time allocation would be necessary for the case presentation and whether any expert evidence would be necessary. Incidentally, the rules of evidence do not apply to mini trials.

In respect of mini trials, time-scheduling is extremely important, including time required for presentations, submissions by advocates and examination of witnesses. The direction hearing therefore becomes extremely important for conducting a mini trial.

There is no point in going into the details of the procedures, but it must be remembered that short-circuiting of the procedure and presentations and submission are the basic aspects of a mini trial. In fact, a mini-trial should be conducted on the basis of essential documents for considering the cases of both parties to a dispute.

8.3 THE CONDUCT OF A MINI TRIAL

A mini trial is conducted in accordance with the procedures and time-table made by the parties themselves, however, the basic procedures that may be followed in conducting a mini trial for any dispute may be summarised. The adviser of the mini trial informs the parties of the procedures and emphasises the importance of confidentiality and the non-binding nature of the process. Of course, the adviser welcomes the parties and expects them to settle their disputes amicably. The claimant's case is presented by its representative; during the presentation of the case he or she may use photographs, tables, films, charts, etc., but the presentation must be completed by the stipulated time. Usually, thereafter, an expert summarises the technical issues on behalf of the claimant and, when necessary, with the help of diagrams and tables clarifies the technical aspects of the issues. After that a key witness may be invited to outline the most important aspects of the claimant's case. The adviser may ask the claimant's representative and witnesses any questions to clarify the case, but the system of cross-examination must not be used. The purpose of asking questions is to clarify certain issues. During this process parties may put their questions, if any, through their advisers or if the agreed procedure permits, directly to the lawyer. The defendant's representative may be permitted to raise certain questions and even if the procedure permits, with the witnesses too.

The defendant's representative then presents the defendant's case in the manner that the claimant's representative presented the claimant's case. In order to maintain the principle of equal opportunities to parties, the defendant's expert will be allowed to summarise the technical issues of the defendant with the aid of films, photos, diagrams etc, if necessary but within the scheduled period of time. The defendant may call a key witness and the neutral expert can ask the defendant's representative and witness any questions that may help clarify the defendant's case. Again, the purpose is not to cross-examine by aggressive means but to seek clarification of issues. Sometimes the agreed procedure allows the expert to have a brief discussion of the issue before the tribunal and thereafter so that claimant's and defendant's representatives will have the opportunity to make their final submissions within the allocated time period. The neutral adviser thereafter adjourns the process in order to allow the parties to discuss the matter further.

8.4 TYPES OF CASES SUITABLE FOR MINI TRIALS

In reality, any matter may be referred to a mini trial, whether it relates to contract, torts, insurance, family issues or construction disputes. Therefore, it would be imprudent to categorically clarify the cases that might be suitable for a mini trial. The purposes of a mini trial are important to bear in mind. Where parties are in a deadlock situation for whatever reason, an outlet to arguing their cases is provided by a mini trial. The advantages of such a trial are that they are less time-consuming and less expensive, and yet allow the parties to know where they stand.

A mini trial may not be suitable for proceedings which would require detailed examination and cross-examination of the witnesses, or where procedures are heavy on points of law.

A mini trial can be held at any stage of a dispute when the representatives are certain that a dispute can be settled without going through lengthy legal proceedings. Of course, the decision of whether a mini trial is preferable can usually be taken after the closing of pleadings and disclosure of documents. In other words, once the representatives have identified the issues, strengths, weaknesses and strategies of the case, a mini trial may be held to test the parties' position and to see whether the dispute may be settled by a fast track procedure. Of course, there is no reason why a mini trial cannot be held at an early stage of a dispute, but probably, it would be appropriate to hold such a trial after the issues and strategies have been identified.

8.5 THE NEUTRAL ADVISER'S POSITION

A neutral adviser, for the purpose of a mini trial, may be a retired judge, a lawyer or any other person familiar with the field of the dispute. He must command respect of the parties. It is not obligatory to appoint a neutral adviser for a mini trial but in most cases it becomes profitable to do so in that neutral advice from an expert certainly puts the parties' issues in the right perspective in order to enable them to assess their respective positions. In other words, it is through a neutral adviser that the parties may obtain an informal view of the merits and weaknesses of the case. It is also through a neutral adviser that contentious issues can be correctly identified and narrowed down to a minimum.

Where a neutral adviser is appointed for conducting a mini trial, he acts as a chairperson and the management of the trial becomes his responsibility.

During the trial he must ensure that he is able to form a view on the basis of the submissions of the parties' representatives but, if necessary, he can also raise questions for clarification of ideas.

After the end of the presentation and submissions of the arguments by both parties the neutral adviser may adjourn the proceedings with a view to discussing issues with the parties and inform the parties of their respective strengths and weaknesses, and what might happen if the case goes to an actual trial. In accordance with the requests of the parties, the neutral adviser will provide either a written and/or oral opinion on the merits of the case on a non-binding basis. The parties will then have an opportunity to discuss their cases even further on the basis of the opinion given by the neutral adviser. But of course, at the request of the parties, the neutral adviser can assist them in negotiating their dispute.

In the United Kingdom, a number of organisations may arrange mini trials and provide neutral advisers, namely, the Centre for Dispute Resolution ("CEDR"), the Chartered Institute of Arbitrators and the British Academy of Experts. Similar organisations exist in many other countries too. It is for the parties to choose an organisation to appoint a neutral adviser or they themselves may appoint an adviser of their own choice without going through an organisation. Where the neutral adviser's intervention does not reach a solution to the dispute, it can be referred to a mediator, but for obvious reasons a neutral adviser in a case cannot be appointed as a mediator for the same case.

In fact, it is through the neutral advisers that alternative dispute resolution methods may be made even more popular and cases of almost all types may be brought under the umbrella of alternative dispute resolution at least for the initial assessments of the merits and weaknesses of the case.

The neutral adviser's role is a crucial one; he is neither a mediator nor a judge; he is merely an informed person in relation to the subject matter of the dispute, and he is primarily endowed with the qualities of being an effective negotiator. He must remain neutral and he must ensure that he is not driven by any bias in favour of or against any party; he must be a friendly and understanding person, and he must command the respect of the parties and the latter must have placed confidence in him. He should obviously be an effective negotiator.

In fact, it is though the neutral advisers that the alternative dispute resolution system may be made even more effective and cases of almost all types may be brought under the umbrella of ADR system, at least for the initial assessments of the merits and weaknesses of the case.

8.6 CONCLUSIONS

A mini trial primarily serves two purposes: (a) it provides a test ground for determining whether a dispute is really triable or not; and it can initiate settlement of disputes after the parties have been informed of the merits and weaknesses of their cases.

Mini trials save costs and time; they are informal and yet they make the parties aware of the nature of their contention and the prospect of winning and losing their cases. But of course the purposes of a mini trial would be defeated if a neutral adviser misdirects the parties. It is therefore essential that advisers to mini trials must be appropriate persons to advise the parties. It is for the adviser to a mini trial to determine what questions should be asked and what clarifications the legal representatives of the parties must provide for a clear understanding of the case. Again, it is for him to make the parties aware of what might happen and in what direction the case might turn if it is referred to an actual trial.

Mini trials are not actual trials. They simply offer the disputants an opportunity to assess their respective position in their case and the risk involved if their case is referred to an actual trial. A mini trial stage represents a screening stage, and the parties, in order to help themselves, should disclose every aspect of their cases in order to enable their advisers to advise them correctly. The outcome of a mini trial might prompt the parties to initiate a negotiated settlement and thus allow them to save cost and time.

It should be emphasised however that in order for a mini trial to be successful, all participants, the parties, their representatives and the neutral adviser must perform their respective role appropriately. Half-hearted efforts made by any of the parties at a mini trial will defeat its purpose.

CHAPTER 9

ADR and Public Policy Issues

9.1 INTRODUCTION

Public policy issues are those issues in which people have a particular interest and the governments are required to take action in order to protect those interests of people. Of course, public policy issues can also be created by the government itself over which people may not have any say, for example, foreign policy issues, foreign investment issues and public finance issues, including taxation. The most popular public issues in the United Kingdom and the United States have been those related to civil rights, housing allocation, planning and land use, environmental and health issues and police and community problems. A community may take special interest in a particular issue and draw the attention of the government by lobbying it through interest groups in order to promote the concern to the status of a public issue.

Co-operative dispute resolution or ADR procedures may prove to be helpful in settling many public policy issues and satisfying the needs of the government and the people. In her analysis, Gail Bingham pointed out that mediation was found to be helpful in the United States in respect of environmental disputes[1]. Again, in the United States mediation of public policy issues has become a common phenomenon; this aspect of dispute settlement is still in its infancy in the United Kingdom.

In this chapter an attempt is made: (a) to identify the reasons for applying ADR in settling public issues; and (b) to consider the appropriateness of ADR in resolving public policy issues.

9.2 REASONS FOR APPLYING FOR SETTLING PUBLIC ISSUES

Public policy issues are those issues which are concerned with public interest such as health, education, welfare, environmental issues and housing. In a democratic society, public policy issues must pay attention to social aspirations. The formation of public policy admits of two approaches:

(a) the initiative that may be taken by a government whether for gaining popularity or for the genuine interest of the society; and

(b) the initiative that may be taken by social groups.

---

[1] See Gail Bingham, *Resolving Environmental Disputes: A Decade of Experience*, (1986) The Conservation Foundation

In the second situation what is to be noticed is whether, in the name of public policy, a particular social group's interest would be more protected than others, but of course, the protection of the interest of such groups is also to be regarded as a dimension to public policy. Broadly speaking, any policy which aims at protecting the interest of the public comes under public policy. Society's participation in public policy issues becomes a common phenomenon in a democratic society when conflicts arise between society's perception of public policy and the government's perception of some. It is to be emphasised however that in a democratic society conflicts between social groups and government authorities must be inevitable and therefore formal structures should be developed and operated.

Cost benefit analysis becomes an important factor for giving rights to conflicts between public policy and social aspiration or when governments without proper democratic procedure wish to adopt controversial procedures which may affect a society's interests. In Great Britain, the introduction of the Community Charge or poll tax during the late 1980s and early 1990s presented conflicts between public policy and social aspirations. The principal aspect of the conflict was the justification for imposing that tax on the basis of the number of adults living in a dwelling. Opposition from the public was so intense that eventually the government was obliged to change the policy, although the current policy on local taxation which is based on the price of property is not sufficiently rational. Such issues may be best settled by conciliation between the government authorities and interest groups.

Conflicts relating to issues of public policy are fit for ADR in that they offer parties opportunities to air their grievances as to the advantages and disadvantages of adopting a policy – there is no reason why court proceedings should be the best means for settling such disputes. The mediation / conciliation procedures might also allow the government to re-consider whether any of its acts may run counter to the public interest; thus it may minimise the incidence of court proceedings in the form of a judicial review.

Conciliation / mediation in respect of public issues has at least two advantages: (a) the public policies may be determined by democratic means; and (b) court proceedings and legal costs may be avoided. This procedure can be applied to any issue of social interest.

In reality, there should not be any conflict between public policy and social aspirations if both parties are prepared to meet for the purposes of conciliation or mediation in the interest of both parties. Conciliation and mediation creates more understanding between the parties.

In this process, however, the strategies and objectives of both parties must be clearly identified. Although initially they may be poles apart, eventually through the conciliation/mediation these differences will be ironed out and the proper policy will be adopted.

Conciliation/mediation may prove to be very effective if only social awareness of issues and policies exists and the society takes the primary initiative to have a balanced view on all matters. It is to be borne in mind that conciliation/mediation is not to be treated in this context as a legal solution to a problem but a societal solution to which a government should conform in order to achieve the maximum benefit for the society. Conciliation/mediation in respect of public issues thus has a social, political and economic dimension. Rapport between social interest groups and governments simply consolidates the current and future position of governments.

9.3 APPROPRIATENESS OF ADR IN RESOLVING PUBLIC POLICY ISSUES

The caution must be entered that although in theory conciliation/mediation about public issues is possible, public policy issues based on the grounds of national interest may not be subject to any conciliation or mediation process. There are certain public policy issues about which the government is not obliged to seek public opinion as to conciliate/mediate, for example, defence related issues, whether or not to maintain diplomatic relations with certain countries. ADR in regard to public policy issues may be possible in respect of matters about which governments, in formulating their policy, may seek public opinion and conciliate in order to adopt a policy which has received a consensus of the public. These issues may be highly politically charged, for example, housing issues, medical facility issues or issues about education.

One should not prescribe ADR for public policy related issues as a matter of practice. The parties need to negotiate an agreement and should consider seriously whether the ground of national interest may be invoked by the government. Public policy mediation should not be initiated without carefully carrying out a fact finding phase to establish its feasibility[2].

In the preparatory stage to ADR for public policy-related issues the following should be considered very seriously:

(a) why is ADR necessary,

(b) whether ADR would produce any realistic results;

(c) who would be the likely parties to the ADR and what would be the nature of their participation;

(d) how many interest groups might be involved in the ADR and whether there would be any prospect of reconciling views of the interest groups;

(e) whether the government may be amenable to these views and the extent to which the government may be prepared to accommodate the view of various interest groups; and

(f) the time-scale for ADR and the cost thereof.

[2] Brown and Marriott, op. cit, at 235

It is important to consider whether the ideas of various groups might be effectively co-ordinated and that they would not lose interest until the ADR has been completed. The nature of commitment on the part of each group must be determined and the time-scale for reaching a conclusion must be notified to them too. These issues are crucially important to ADR in respect of public policy issues which require elaborate information gathering, time and funds. They also require the engagement of a large number of researchers and other workers. In carrying out ADR in public policy-related issues, attention should be paid to the issue of disclosure, that is, whether public authorities may claim privilege whereby information may be withheld on valid grounds.

Before carrying out ADR it is also to be ensured that co-operation from all the interest groups would be available and that they should remain within the ADR process until its closure. Furthermore, attendance of vital witnesses from various groups becomes an important factor in order to make ADR in respect of public policy-related issues a success.

It must also be ensured whether the differing interests of different interest groups may jeopardise ADR in respect of public policy-related issues, in other words, there must be an identity of common problems and issues, and a determination on the part of the action groups to oppose a public policy in a co-ordinated and united fashion. In order to sustain their case, interest groups are often required to seek expert reports and the opposition must ensure that they have sufficient funds to carry out ADR. The issue of funding is fundamentally important in that quite often private parties are unable to afford to carry out action against a public body.

In order to make ADR successful in respect of public policy three points are extremely important: (a) whether the matter can be referred to ADR over a short period of time so that the interest of the action group remains live; (b) the funding does not run out; and (c) the level of co-operation remains intact.

9.4 CONDITIONS TO BE SATISFIED FOR ADR IN REGARD TO PUBLIC POLICY ISSUES

Public policy issue related disputes are by nature complex; they embrace a number of issues. The duty to protect the interests of all probable parties presents difficulty in having a balanced and just conclusion. Before embarking upon the ADR process it would be advisable to carry out some preparatory work, and a list of items which should be considered at the preparatory stage is given below:

(a) The selection procedures of conciliators must be determined ensuring that they are not questioned by any of the parties involved in ADR and also that parties place their confidence in the chosen experts. The conciliators must also be familiar with the public policy issues with which the dispute is concerned.

(b) The time-scale for ADR and the sources of funds must be determined. In fact, if this issue is not settled, there is little point in proposing ADR at all because the public body concerned will not be short of funds; thus in the absence of sufficient funds, the private parties may need to surrender in the middle of mediation.

(c) Clarity of issues is fundamentally important because otherwise time will be spent unproductively. In regard to this matter intervention by lawyers may be useful as most public policy issues have legal implications. Furthermore, an agenda is essential at an early stage of ADR; otherwise, the ADR process will not proceed according to any framework.

(d) The manner in which parties would be required to participate in ADR process is crucially important; therefore the parties may have to be briefed in sufficient time. Social implications of public policy issues being fundamental in nature, each party to public policy-related ADR process must be well informed and articulate in upholding the social cause; otherwise the purpose of ADR will be defeated, and unbriefed parties might also present difficulty for the conciliator to exercise sufficient control over the ADR process.

(e) In public policy-related ADR, conciliators must be able to appreciate the public interest issues and public policies issues; their function is not necessarily to support the cause of the minority; on the other hand, they must also ensure that the majority view receives appropriate attention. Public policy-related ADR has gained grounds in the United States, and it is acknowledged that this type of ADR represents a wide range of interests and the tasks of mediators have become extremely complex[3]

An ADR expert must have to be skilled in negotiating techniques; he must also be dynamic and develop creative solutions[4]. It is to be considered whether instead of appointing one conciliator, two or three should be appointed in dealing with complex public policy related ADRs. Take, for example, ADR with regard to environmental issues – on the one hand, the government has an obligation to secure the protection of the environment by regulatory means, on the other hand, governmental action might prove to be financially burdensome for the business community. A conciliator is therefore required to perform a balancing act whereby the interests of both parties will be protected and also whereby the government would realise the type of action that may be required to be taken in the future in regard to the matter concerned.

[3] See further "The Policy Dialague: Applying Mediation to the Policy-Making Process" by John R Ehrmann and Michael T Lesnick in (1988) 20 M. Q. 93–99

[4] See further Susskind and Cruikshank (1987) *Breaking the Impasse: Consensual Approaches to Resolving Public Disputes*, and Christopher W Moore (1986) *The Mediation Process*

A complex ADR process therefore involves a variety of stages: identification and examination of the issues with the help of the parties, designing the process, scheduling the procedure, the agenda building and finally, the actual process of reaching an agreement between the parties[5]. One of the means of avoiding a lengthy ADR process is to initiate a public inquiry by a neutral expert body and to consider the views of the experts by both parties. The hearings of report inquiry must be informal and must take place in the presence of an inspector. Such a system is available in relation to town and country planning matters. The inspector who acts as a mediator discusses the issues with the interested parties and he defines the areas of conflict. At such informal meetings the mediation process takes place indirectly and proves to be helpful in that both parties may decide to reconsider their respective positions. The caution must be entered, however, that this process does not take the form of an adjudication. In the United Kingdom public inquiries often take the form of adjudications and it is operated in a very formal manner, often with legal representations. Perhaps any informal, non-binding discussion of the inquiry stage based on expert's opinions would be much more useful in settling a dispute. Of course, for the sake of neutrality, each party should be asked to submit expert reports.

Again, for example, whether a bus lane would be useful in a residential area and whether it would jeopardise the interest of small business in the street can be resolved by informal inquiries based on expert reports and then formalisation of it by ADR.

9.5 CONCLUSIONS

Research has been carried out in the United States to establish the nature of effectiveness of public issue related mediations[6]. The results produced by Bingham are interesting in that whereas according to him the high rate of success in reaching agreements became evident, the rate of implementation was rather low. Bingham also found that implementation of public policy related mediations was more successful in relation to site-related issues. Whatever may be the result in the US, it is maintained that public attitude towards ADR is an important factor for considering whether the American process should be followed in the United Kingdom. By coincidence however public inquiry system has become more prevalent in the construction and building industries and perhaps in the road traffic sector in the UK.

Public policy-related ADR should attract the attention of the public more when they are likely to appreciate the effect of intended government planning. In other words, the interest of the public might not be prevalent in an appreciable manner if the subject-matter of the mediation is not regarded to

[5] See further Ehrmann and Lesnick

[6] See further Gail Bingham, *Resolving Environmental Disputes: A Decade of Experience* (1986) and Philip J Harter, *Negotiating Regulations: A Cure for Malaise*, 71 Georgetown L.J. (1982).

be sufficient for public interest. A degree of awareness of the rights of the public is essential in initiating mediation / conciliation procedure in public policy-related issues. A degree of imbalance in the decision-making process might take place in that the public body may sometimes exercise an over-powering attitude. It is therefore for the mediator / conciliator to tackle that problem. In a democratic society there is no reason why mediation / conciliation procedure should not be encouraged to operate in resolving public policy-related issues.

CHAPTER 10

Certain Mediation Systems

10.1 INTRODUCTION

It is thought appropriate to examine and evaluate mediation systems operated under the auspices of certain institutions, which are of a truly international or national character. The chosen institutions are: The World Intellectual Property Organisation (WIPO); the Centre for Effective Dispute Resolution (CEDR); the London Court of International Arbitration (LCIA), and the Stockholm Chamber of Commerce Mediation Institute.

10.2 THE WORLD INTELLECTUAL PROPERTY ORGANISATION (WIPO) MEDIATION SYSTEM

WIPO has established an arbitration and mediation centre and has adopted its own mediation rules. It is possible for parties to combine mediation with arbitration under the WIPO Rules. When these two methods of settling disputes are combined, the dispute is submitted first under the WIPO Mediation Rules and, in the event of failing to reach a settlement within a defined period of time (usually within 60 or 90 days), or where a party refuses to participate or continue in the mediation, the dispute is referred to arbitration for a binding decision under the WIPO Arbitration Rules.

By agreeing to submit a dispute to WIPO Mediation, the parties are governed by the WIPO Mediation Rules as part of their agreement to mediate. The WIPO Mediation and Arbitration Centre offers specialised services for mediation of disputes pertaining to intellectual property or commercial transactions and relationships involving the exploitation of intellectual property. Disputes relate to matters ranging between know-how, patents and trade mark licences, franchises, computer contracts, technology-related employment contracts, publishing, music and film contracts and any other matter in which intellectual property rights may be involved.

A mediator appointed under the WIPO Mediation Rules has the mandate to deal with all aspects of any dispute. The WIPO Mediation and Arbitration system is one which is governed by an independent administrative authority with specialised expertise in intellectual property. The mediators and arbitrators include individuals with specialised knowledge and experience in the subject-matter of intellectual property in addition to possessing experience in international commercial arbitration. It is a flexible system and the structure of mediation is very much chosen by the parties with the mediator who also agrees the procedure which is to be followed.

After being appointed, the mediator conducts a series of initial discussions with the parties whether by correspondence or otherwise during which time a schedule for a mediation process is determined, and the mediator indicates what documents he might need prior to his first meeting with the parties. The mediator is required to establish with the parties at the first meeting the ground rules that will be followed in the mediation process. The agenda and schedule of the meetings are also established at the first meeting. The mediator further ensures that the parties understand the rules of mediation, including the rules on confidentiality set out in the WIPO Mediation Rules. At this meeting, the mediator also requests the parties to provide any other documents that he might need should he require the assistance of experts. The mediation under the WIPO Rules may be of two types: (a) facilitative and (b) evaluative. At the first meeting, it will also be clear whether the mediator is taking a facilitative role and, if so, it will entail the following steps:

(a) collection of information concerning the dispute and the identification of the issues involved;

(b) identification of the parties' interests, the nature of their grievances and the remedies they seek; and

(c) the development of strategies and options that might satisfy the parties.

At this stage the mediator also explains the merits and disadvantages of mediation, court proceedings and arbitration. Throughout a mediation, however, private consultations with the mediator, experts and the representatives of the parties are allowed to continue. The following are the principal stages under the WIPO Mediation system:

(a) the agreement to mediate;

(b) submission of a Request for Mediation;

(c) appointment of the mediator;

(d) setting up of the first meeting;

(e) setting up of subsequent meetings; and

(f) reaching an agreement.

At subsequent meetings, however, the parties are required to agree to the ground rules of the mediation process, identifying the issues, exploring the interest of the parties and developing options for settlement. The language of the mediation is chosen by the parties themselves and where more than one language is to be used provision for an interpreter is made and the cost thereof is to be borne by the parties themselves.

The WIPO Mediation and Arbitration Centre assists parties in identifying and agreeing upon a mediator. The Centre submits the biographical details of potential mediators. It is for the parties to choose independently their mediator(s). Where the parties have very different cultural and linguistic backgrounds they may want to nominate co-mediators.

The WIPO Centre performs the following functions as an administrative authority of the mediation:

(a) assists the parties in selecting and appointing a mediator;

(b) fixes, in consultation with the parties and the mediator, the fees of the mediator;

(c) requires the parties to submit an agreed deposit and fixes the time by which the remainder of the fees of the mediator must be paid and the fees of the interpreter, if any, and

(d) provides facilities for mediation including translation and secretarial services.

It is for the parties to decide the location of mediation as the process need not necessarily take place at the Centre where the headquarters of WIPO are located.

In respect of any mediation a registration fee must be paid to the Centre which amount to 10% of the value in dispute up to a maximum of US$10,000 which is charged when the amount in dispute is US$10,000,000. The mediator's fee may be negotiated but it is usually calculated on an hourly or daily basis, bearing in mind his/her experience. Under the WIPO Mediation Rules (Article 24) the registration fee of the Centre, the mediator's fees and all his/her other expenses must be borne in equal shares by the parties. The parties have, however, the freedom to change the allocation of costs.

The Centre has developed a recommended contract clause for the reference of future disputes under a contract to mediate under the WIPO Mediation Rules. It has also adopted a recommended submission agreement for the reference of the existing dispute to mediation under the WIPO Mediation Rules.

10.2.1 An Examination of the WIPO Mediation Rules

A mediation process under the WIPO System may be initiated either by means of an agreement between the parties to submit a dispute to mediation which clause may be embodied in the relevant contract or by agreeing to submit a dispute to mediation after the dispute has actually arisen. At both instances the parties are required to send to the Centre a Request for Mediation detailing the nature of the dispute, the parties to the dispute and their representatives, if any.

By submitting a dispute to the Centre the parties agree to be governed by the Mediation Rules of the Centre although a confirmation of this may be made in the contract itself. The Mediation Rules of the WIPO Centre, which were adopted in 1994, consist of 27 Articles and a Schedule of Fees. The contents of these Rules are now summarised.

Under the WIPO Rules a *"mediation agreement"* means:

> *". . . an agreement by the parties to submit to mediation all or certain disputes which have arisen or which may arise between them; a Mediation Agreement may be in the form of a mediation clause in a contract or in the form of a separate agreement."*[1]

"Submission" in this context would mean submission as it is understood in the case of arbitrations but the term *"disputes"* will have a different meaning in this context because disputes may and generally should include differences. In the case of an arbitration a dispute may stand for a justiciable dispute but the primary purpose of encouraging the parties to come to mediation is to settle their differences without giving special importance to the legal aspects of a dispute. From this standpoint perhaps Article 1 should have provided for *"differences"* also. The WIPO Mediation Rules directly or indirectly encourage parties to include a mediation clause in a contract along the lines of an arbitration clause or a general dispute settlement clause. This has an advantage in that in drafting the underlying contract the parties or their lawyers in drafting the main commercial contract should bear in mind mediation as a method of setting disputes and incorporate this alternative into the contract. Article 1 of the Rules is comprehensive in that if a contract does not contain a mediation clause the parties can still refer their dispute to the WIPO Mediation Centre provided that mediation as a manner of settling disputes has been accepted by the parties in the form of a separate contract. Under the WIPO Mediation Rules the parties can appoint either a sole mediator or more than one mediator. Future disputes under a contract may also be included for submission to the WIPO Mediation Centre. Under Article 1 the parties have the right to submit to mediation all or certain disputes which have arisen or may arise under a contract. In summary, the basis for referring a dispute to the WIPO Mediation Centre is either that a mediation clause has been incorporated into the contract or that a separate contract has been concluded for that purpose.

Article 2 of the Mediation Rules refers to their scope of application. If a mediation agreement provides for mediation under the WIPO Mediation Rules then these rules must be deemed to form part of the Mediation Agreement. In other words, if the parties agree to refer their disputes to the WIPO Mediation mechanism they must accept the WIPO Mediation Rules, and these rules shall apply as from the date of a Request for Mediation of a dispute

[1] Mediation Rules, Article 1 at http://www.arbiter.wipo.int/mediation/mediation-rules/index.html

to WIPO mediation process. All requests for mediation must be submitted to the Centre in writing and a copy of the Request for Mediation must be sent to the other party.

10.2.2 Examples of Panel Decision rendered by the WIPO Arbitration and Mediation Centre

Sydney Opera House Trust v Trilynx Pty. Limited, Case No. D2000-1224

Sydney Opera House Trust of Sydney Opera House, the claimant, brought an action against Trilynx Pty Ltd, the respondent on the disputed domain name – sydneyoperahouse.net, and the register of which was Netware Solutions Inc. of Hudson, Virgina, USA.

This was an administrative proceedings pursuant to the Uniform Domain Name Dispute Resolution Policy adopted by the Internet Corporation for Assigned Names and Numbers (ICANN) on 26 August 1999[2]. The response to the complaint was received by the stipulated date. The Centre duly invited Mr Alan Limbury to serve as a panelist and the latter, who accepted the invitation, was duly appointed.

Facts of the Case

The complainant was appointed manager and administrator of the Sydney Opera House, this post included duties that might be appropriate to the profitable and effective attainment of its *"objects and performance of its functions."* To this end, the Sydney Opera House Trust was specifically authorised *"to register, purchase or apply for or otherwise acquire any trademark which may seem capable of being used in the exercise or in furtherance of any of its functions or the acquisition of which may seem to be calculated directly or indirectly to benefit the Trust."*[3]

Sydney Opera House Trust was also the registered proprietor in Australia of the trademark *"Sydney Opera House"*, in addition to having it registered in Japan. The complainant licensed the use of its trademark. The respondent who is specialised in building *"Web networks"* also owned the domain holdings, including the disputed domain name, which was registered on 6 May 1999. The respondent did not apply to register a trademark incorporating the mark *Sydney Opera House* nor any similar business name. The respondent was not only in the business of developing web and card technologies, but also a proprietor of various websites, including the disputed domain name; they did not however apply to register a trademark incorporating the mark *"Sydney Opera House"* nor any similar business name.

[2] The Policy should be read with the Rules for the Policy adopted by ICANN on 24 October 1991 and the Supplemental Rules for the Policy of the WIPO Arbitration and Mediation Centre.

[3] See p 2 of the Panel Decision

The Parties' Contentions

The complainant maintained that the domain name was similar to its famous mark "*Sydney Opera House*", an internationally-known institution. As the respondent was not authorised by the complainant to use the latter's trademark or its domain name, therefore the respondent had no legitimate interest in that name. Any use by the respondent of the disputed domain name in relation to goods or services would infringe the complainant's rights and contravene the consumer protection provisions of the Australian Trade Practices Act 1974, and any attempt at the commercial use of the domain name would not be made in good faith. Even though no active use of the domain name was made, its registration by an entity with no affiliation with the complainant would have constituted bad faith registration and use.

The main name "*Sydney Opera House*" became famous not by virtue of the merchandise but rather by virtue of its cultural heritage – a symbol of Australia and Sydney. In maintaining its argument the respondent relied on the definition of World Heritage provided by UNESCO:

> "*What make the concept of World Heritage exceptional in its universal application. World Heritage sites belong to all the peoples of the world, irrespective of the territory on which they are located.*"

Buildings of global significance are "*recognised generically in nature*"; Sydney Opera House was not made famous because of the complainant's activities and trademark rights in merchandising products for the Australian and Japanese tourist markets. The respondent questioned the allegation of confusing similarity; furthermore, it maintained that the disputed domain name was different from the complainant's official websites address; and that the respondent's business was totally different from that of the complainant. By referring to the extent of its business, and its owning of a large number of generic domain buildings, and that its interests are to build global community work, the respondent attempted to establish that it has a legitimate interest in the dispute.

The other important arguments put forward by the respondent were:

(i) that it has rights under the United Nations accord for self-determination, which allows it to consider its position as a "*protectionist*"; and that it was through its action that the respondent was able to prevent a possible escalation of damage;

(ii) that there was no point in the respondent's developing or linking the disputed domain because of his future plan to launch a "*global network*", using its own domains; meanwhile, no evidence was submitted by the complainant to prove the allegation that the respondent could be accused of "*passive use*" of the domain name;

(iii) that in the absence of sustainable evidence, the proceedings were brought in bad faith by the complainant.

Discussion and Findings

According to the Panel, in order to qualify for cancellation or transfer, a complainant would be required to prove the following:

(a) that the disputed domain name was identical or confusingly similar to a trademark or service mark in which the complainant had rights;

(b) that the respondent had no rights or legitimate interest in respect of the domain name;

(c) that the registered disputed domain was being used in bad faith.[4]

The Panel considered each of these issues separately by referring to the Policy which has not been annexed to the Decision. However, according to the Panel, by virtue of its objects, functions and powers conferred on the complainant by statute, it was entitled to use a common law trademark and to register the name Sydney Opera House; thus the complainant had rights in that mark. Furthermore, even essential identity would be sufficient for satisfying the criterion of *"identical"* or *"confusing similarity"*. The NSW Parliament, on behalf of the people of New South Wales, designated the complainant as the appropriate entity to manage and administer the famous building and protect its reputation. Despite the fact that the respondent had every good intention of becoming a responsible owner of the disputed domain name and would prevent others from significantly damaging the cultural heritage of the peoples, the law of New South Wales prevented the respondent from establishing a legitimate right or interest in the domain name. In this case, the reputation of the Sydney Opera House was enough to identify the building; there was every need to protect the name, and the respondent might not be aware that the complainant had registered the name as a trademark and might not have appreciated that the complainant had common law rights in the name[5]. The respondent should have known the provisions of the Sydney Opera House Trust Act 1961 (NSW); furthermore, Parliament entrusted to the complainant the maintenance and administration of the building and the protection of any trademark the complainant might acquire or register to meet its objects[6].

The use of the domain name must have been intended by the respondent to create an impression that it was the *"official"* protector of the name of the Opera House.

The Panel therefore decided that the domain name must be transferred to the complainant.

Plan Express Inc v Plan Express, WIPO Arbitration and Mediation Centre, Decision of the Administrative Panel, Case No. D2000-0565

---

[4] See p 4 of the Panel Decision

[5] op. cit., at p 4

[6] ibid.

Facts of the Case

Plan Express Inc, a corporation organised under the laws of the State of Wisconsin, USA, having its principal place of business in Memphis, Tennessee, submitted a complaint against Plan Express (the respondent), a Texas corporation in Houston, on the ground that the respondent registered as a domain name a mark which was identical to the service mark registered and used by the complainant, and that it used the domain name in bad faith. The dispute was submitted to the WIPO Arbitration and Mediation Centre.

The domain name *"planexpress.com"* was registered with the US Patent Office on 12 October 1999. The complainant operated under the domain name since 1994. The respondents had the domain name registered (April 1998) when, as it alleged, it was unaware of the existence of the business operating under the name *"Plan Express in Memphis"*. The respondents demonstrated by evidence that it expended funds in order to develop a website prior to the complainant lodging its complaint. The respondent, who ultimately ceased all development of the website owing to financial reasons, virtually sold the domain name to a third party. The sale was on hold pending resolution of this dispute.

The Issues

The complainant contended that the respondent registered as a domain name a mark which was identical to the service mark registered and used by the complainant; therefore the respondent had no rights or legitimate interests in respect of the domain name at issue, and the respondent used the domain name in bad faith.

The respondent, on the other hand, contended that the domain name at issue was not identical or confusingly similar to complainant's trademark, and that it has a right or legitimate interest in respect of the domain name. Furthermore, the respondent neither registered nor used the domain name in bad faith. The respondent sought a determination that the complainant acted in bad faith.

Discussion of the Issues

The principal issues were:

(a) whether the domain name registered by the respondent was identical or confusingly similar to a trademark or service mark;

(b) whether the respondent had any legitimate interest in respect of the domain name; and

(c) whether the domain name was registered and used in bad faith.

The Panel found in favour of the respondent on the grounds that:

(a) the domain name was identical or confusingly similar to the domain name at issue;

(b) that by means of evidence it was established that the respondent registered the domain name prior to the application by the complainant to register its trademark;

(c) the Tribunal was satisfied that during the material period, that is, the time in dispute, the respondent started developing a website using the domain name at issue;

(d) that as the respondent had a right or legitimate interest in the domain name at issue, there was no need to determine whether the respondent had registered the domain name.

10.2.3 The Request for Mediation

A Request for Mediation initiates the mediation process. It must contain the names, addresses, telephones, telex, telefax and other methods of communication numbers (presumably email) of the parties to a dispute in addition to containing the names of the representatives of the party filing the Request for Mediation. A Request for Mediation must also be accompanied by a mediation agreement and a brief statement of the nature of the dispute. The rationale for submitting a copy of the mediation agreement is to justify the reason for referring a dispute to the WIPO Mediation process. The statement explaining the nature of a dispute must identify the basis for the dispute and the legal issues arising therefrom, in addition to identifying the nature of remedies sought. The date of commencement of mediation is the date on which the Request for Mediation is received by the Centre; in other words, the date of posting the Request has no relevance to the date of commencement.

The Centre is required to notify the other party of the date on which the Request for Mediation is received. This has a bearing upon the future scheduling of the stages of a mediation process. It is not clear from the Rules whether receipt of the Request for Mediation by fax or email will be regarded as the date of receipt for the purposes of the commencement date or whether the Centre would wait for the hard copy of the communication to come through. The Rules do not provide for rejection of a Request for Mediation. It is not clear what would happen if a Request for Mediation sent to the Centre was not correctly formulated. In that event it is assumed that the date of commencement should be the date when the corrected and acceptable version is received by the Centre.

10.2.4 Appointment of the Mediator

Articles 6, 7 and 8 of the Rules are concerned with the appointment of mediators. Parties have the right to nominate their mediator(s). Where parties have not exercised their right the Centre shall appoint the mediator(s) after consultation with the parties. Consultation with the parties is essential in order to ensure that they will have confidence in the mediator(s) including their competence. In other words, consent is the basis for the appointment of mediators. It is assumed that mediators, when nominated by the Centre, will be individuals of acknowledged competence in respect of the issues with which a dispute is concerned. Whether a mediator is nominated by the parties themselves or by the Centre, an offer of the appointment must be made to him and, if he accepts it, he is then deemed to have undertaken to make available sufficient time in order to ensure that mediation is conducted expeditiously. This point is particularly important because otherwise a quick or fast-track method of setting disputes through a mediation period will be defeated. The mediator is required to give an undertaking that he will have sufficient time to devote himself to mediation; this point is also important because many professional mediators are often overbooked in consequence of which an expeditious settlement of disputes may not take place. At the time of accepting an appointment a mediator is required to pay attention to this important issue bearing in mind that the parties will be spending money not only for a satisfactory settlement but also for an expeditious process.

A mediator must be neutral, impartial and independent. In this regard there is no fundamental difference between the qualities of a mediator or of a judge. However, a mediator must be reminded of these qualities in case he is persuaded by arguments put forward by a stronger party, such as a corporate body or a government department. Of course, experienced mediators will necessarily satisfy these qualities and criteria.

10.2.5 Representation of Parties and Participation in Meetings

Under the WIPO Rules the parties may be represented or assisted in their meetings with each other or the mediators; however, it is possible for the parties to represent their cases personally. Where, however, representatives are appointed, their names, addresses and the party on whose behalf a representative will be acting must be communicated to both parties, the mediator and the Centre. Article 8 of the Rules simply states "*... persons authorised to represent a party*"; it is assumed that individuals with legal background or practising lawyers in any jurisdiction may be allowed to act as persons authorised to represent a party. This point is important in that a mediator may be involved in dealing with legal issues. Even where a mediator is predominantly concerned with facts, the parties may prefer to appoint persons with legal background to represent their cases.

10.2.6 Role of the Mediator

In this connection the reader's attention is drawn to the discussion in Chapter 7 of this work in which the role of a mediator has been critically examined. The

WIPO Rules have also included the qualities that should be found in a mediator. However, the WIPO Rules specifically state that:

> *"The mediator shall promote the settlement of the issues in dispute between the parties in any manner that the mediator believes to be appropriate, but shall have no authority to impose a settlement on the parties."*[7]

Thus a mediator is required to promote *"a settlement of the issues in dispute between the parties"*. In other words, he must have the qualities which will allow him to promote the settlement rather than remaining present at mediation as an innocent by-stander. He must have a clear idea of the issues in dispute between the parties in order to be able to promote settlement of the issues. The WIPO Rules provide mediation with a wide discretion to determine and apply the procedure that, in his opinion, is the most appropriate in a given case in promoting settlement of the issues in dispute. The Rules enter the caution, however, that a mediator shall have no authority to impose a settlement on the parties. The WIPO Rules stress that settlement of the dispute must be reached primarily through the interaction between the parties by gradual process whereby the misunderstandings and differences will be eliminated. A mediator would be acting primarily as a referee.

Under the WIPO Rules, if it appears to a mediator that any issues in the dispute between the parties are not susceptible to resolution through mediation, he may then propose to the parties procedures or means for resolving these issues having regard to the circumstances of the dispute. The parties have the discretion either to accept or reject the suggested procedures or means for resolving these issues. A mediator might also propose an expert determination of more specialised issues or arbitration. In other words, the mediator under the WIPO Rules, like rules of many other institutions, has an obligation to draw the attention of the parties at an early stage to whether mediation would be the most appropriate method of settling certain issues of the dispute as a whole. Where, however, a mediation process might turn out to be another lengthy process he should advise the parties of the method which would lead to the most efficient, least costly and most productive settlement of the contentious issues. A mediator may also propose the submission of last offers of settlement by each party and in the absence of any settlement through mediation, arbitration would be conducted on the basis of those last offers of settlement by each party. This will enable the arbitral tribunal to confine its remit to determining which of the last offers should prevail. Alternatively, with the consent of the parties, the mediator might direct the dispute to arbitration in which he will act as the sole arbitrator. The WIPO Rules thus admit of a progression in the role of a mediator, that is, from the position of a mediator to that of an arbitrator. The advantages of this progression are twofold:

---

[7] Article 13(a) of the WIPO Rules

(a) that the mediator's role would then be transferred into the role of an arbitrator who will be acting in accordance with the usual authority that an arbitrator enjoys in an international arbitration; and

(b) that being conversant with the issues he should be able to short-circuit many items and get into the principal issues quickly. This should be regarded as another time-saving and cost-saving procedure.

10.2.7 Conduct of Mediation

The manner in which mediation shall be conducted is agreed by the parties. Should the parties fail to reach an agreement on this matter, the mediator shall, in accordance with the Rules, prescribe the manner in which the mediation will be conducted. One of the conditions of activating mediation under the WIPO Rules is that each party *"shall co-operate in good faith with the mediator to advance the need as expeditiously as possible"*[8]. The term *"good faith"* has in this context a contractual element in that good faith forms a foundation of all contracts. Therefore, the parties are required in advance to give an unconditional guarantee that they would co-operate in progressing mediation as expeditiously as possible.

The mediator is free to meet and communicate separately with a party on *a without prejudice* basis, that is, such communication shall not be disclosed to the other party unless the latter by express authorisation allows disclosure of such information. Communication in private with the parties individually is crucially important because the mediator through such meetings gains more insight into the causes of the dispute and so the parties feel comfortable in discussing their grievances with the mediator. Such meetings effectively curtail the duration of the mediation process but on the other hand, disclosure of the outcome of discussions held in private with appropriate authorisation of the party concerned may also heighten the conclusion process by narrowing down the differences between the parties.

However, soon after he is appointed, the mediator shall, in consultation with the parties, set a time-table for the submission by each party to mediation of statements summarising the background to the dispute, the details of the claims and evidence in support of claims. The mediator has the right to ask a party during the mediation process to provide such additional information or materials as he may deem useful. On the other hand, the parties are free to submit to the mediator at any stage any written information or materials of a confidential nature for consideration by the mediator only. Again, without any written authorisation by the party concerned, the mediator shall not disclose such information or materials to the other party.

In this regard the WIPO Mediation System follows the general pattern of mediation in the commercial world, that is, it is operative at sessions of

[8] Article 10

meetings of both a public and a private nature. The reasons for conducting confidential meetings are twofold:

(a) To enlighten the mediator as to the issues or fundamental route of dissension which perhaps cannot be disclosed in writing or if certain other information would be necessary in order to supplement the knowledge of the mediator about the dispute and through such meetings confidence in the mediator is further developed.

(b) On the other hand, if the parties should initially fail to develop any confidence in their mediator for whatever reason, there will be no need for any private meetings between the parties and the mediator and therefore effectively the mediation process will come to an end.

10.2.8 Confidentiality

In order to allow parties to maintain their confidence in the mediation process, under the WIPO Rules, recording of any kind of any meetings of the parties with the mediator is impermissible. This confidentiality rule also applies to any party, namely the representatives of and advisors to the parties, any independent expert or any other person who may be present at any meetings of the parties with the mediator, and *"unless otherwise agreed by the parties and the mediator, use or disclose to any outside party any information concerning, or obtained in the course of the mediation."*[9] Any person who may be involved in the mediation process is required to sign an appropriate confidentiality undertaking prior to taking part in the mediation.

Under the WIPO Rules, the issue of confidentiality is vitally important. Unless otherwise agreed by the parties, each person involved in the mediation is required, on the termination of the mediation, to return to the party that may have provided them any documents or materials. Furthermore, notes taken by an individual of any meetings of the parties with the mediator must be destroyed on the termination of the mediation.

Unless otherwise agreed by the parties neither the mediator nor the parties shall introduce as evidence in any judicial or arbitral proceedings any views expressed or suggestions put forward by a party with regard to the possible settlement of the dispute or any submission made by a party during the course of the mediation process or any proposals made or expressed by the mediator in an attempt to resolve a dispute or the fact that a party had or had not agreed to accept any proposal for settlement made by the mediator or by the other party[10]. Disclosure of any such information may prejudice judicial or arbitral proceedings if the parties should decide to refer their dispute to these.

---

[9] Article 15

[10] Article 17

10.2.9 Termination of Mediation

Under the WIPO Rules mediation shall be terminated either by the signing of a settlement agreement by the parties or by the decision of a mediator that it would be inappropriate to proceed with the mediation process any further as it is unlikely to lead to a resolution of a dispute or by written declaration of a party at any time after attending the first meeting of the parties with the mediator but before the signing of any settlement agreement. In other words, mediation may also be terminated by the parties at any stage of the mediation process. It is for a prudent mediator to ensure during the initial stage that likelihood of continuity with a mediation will result in a resolution of the dispute.

However, upon the termination of a mediation process, the mediator shall promptly send to the Centre a notice of termination including the date on which it is effectively terminated whether or not mediation resulted in settlement of the dispute in full or partially. The mediator shall also send a copy of the termination notice addressed to the Centre to the parties concerned. The Centre shall keep the termination notice confidential unless disclosure of the notice is authorised by the parties. The Centre does not publish any information which would reveal the identity of the parties although it may include information concerning the information in any aggregate statistical data that it may publish pertaining to its activities.

Unless required by a court of law or authorised in writing by the parties, a mediator shall not act in any capacity whatsoever in any proceedings current or future, judicial or arbitral or otherwise related to the subject-matter of the dispute.

10.2.10 Other Issues[11]

The Request for Mediation must be registered with the Internal Bureau of the WIPO and the registration fee is payable in accordance with the Schedule of Fees applicable on the date of the Request for Mediation. Mediation cannot be activated unless the registration fee has been paid within 15 days of the second reminder in writing from the Centre to pay the registration fee.

The mediator's fees in the currency in which fees are to be paid and the time by which they must be paid are all settled in consultation with the parties and the mediator. Unless the parties and the mediator agree otherwise the amount of the fees is calculated on an hourly basis or in accordance with the daily indicative rates set in the Schedule of Fees, taking into account the amount of claims, the complexity of the dispute and any other relevant circumstances of the case[12]. At the time of appointing a mediator the Centre may require each party to deposit an equal amount as the advance for the cost of mediation including in particular the estimated fees of the mediator and the other

[11] Article 21

[12] Article 22

expenses that may be incurred during the mediation. Incidentally, in the case of arbitration conducted by the International Chamber of Commerce a deposit must be paid in advance. Supplementary deposits will be required to be paid by the parties if the Centre so directs them. If the required deposit is not paid within 15 days of the second reminder in writing from the Centre, the Request for Mediation is deemed to have been terminated, and the Centre shall notify all parties concerned accordingly. After the termination of mediation, the Centre returns any unexpected balance to the parties, or conversely may require the parties to make extra payments, if necessary. Unless otherwise agreed with the parties, the registration fee, mediator's fee and other expenses that may be incurred by the mediator including his travelling expenses and expenses incurred for obtaining expert advice are to be borne in equal shares by the parties.

In regard to exclusion of liability Article 25 of the WIPO Rules provides that:

> *"Except in respect of deliberate wrongdoing, the mediator, WIPO and the Center shall not be liable to any party for any act or omission in connection with any mediation conducted under these Rules."*

The parties, the mediator, representatives of the parties and anybody else concerned with the mediation must give a waiver of defamation whereby no action for defamation, slander or any related complaint can be brought against any of them for any statement or comments, whether oral or written, made or used by them in preparation for or in the course of mediation. Mediations under the WIPO Rules are not subject to any statutes of limitation or equivalent law.

The amount of the registration fee shall be 0.10% of the value of the claim but the maximum registration fee cannot exceed US$10,000. Where a Request for Mediation does not indicate any claims in monetary claims or where a dispute is not quantifiable in monetary terms, a registration fee of US$750 is payable subject to adjustment, that is, adjustment which is achieved after consultation with the parties and the mediator. All monetary amounts must be expressed in US dollars.

10.2.11 Conclusions

WIPO clauses are often used in agreements concluded between parties from different jurisdictions. The WIPO procedures may be used for all types of commercial disputes, be they intellectual property-related or otherwise. WIPO clauses are also found in licensing agreements; such as information technology licences, franchising and merchandising agreements involving trademarks, transfer agreements relating to patents or manufacturing know-how, and agreements pertaining to entertainment industry products.

There exists a standard clause for each of the procedures administered by the Centre. The Centre's legal staff offer free drafting advice. The Centre also works with intellectual property-related organisations and industries to cater for their needs in regard to dispute resolution.

WIPO has also developed a Uniform Domain Name Dispute Resolution Policy which was adopted by the Internet Corporation for Assigned Names and Numbers (ICANN), and the Rules for Uniform Domain Name Dispute Resolution Policy (the "Rules") both of which were adopted on 24 October 1999. A discussion of these documents is beyond the remit of this work.

10.3 THE CENTRE FOR EFFECTIVE DISPUTE RESOLUTION (CEDR)

Centre for Effective Dispute Resolution ("CEDR") has developed model clauses which parties desiring to settle by mediation may decide to accept or they may even devise their own clauses. However, if a party has decided to adopt the CEDR model it is expected that in the event of a dispute arising under a contract mediation it will be governed by the CEDR Rules. In February 1999 CEDR adopted a Model Mediation Procedure and Agreement including guidance notes, and in September 1999 it also adopted Model ADR Contract Clauses. A brief summary of these documents is now given. It is not necessary to go through all the clauses of the Model Mediation Procedure and Agreement because if parties should decide to be governed by CEDR Mediation Procedures, they will automatically accept the Procedure and Agreement developed by CEDR.

CEDR takes the role of an administrator whose role includes a number of functions, for example, subject to agreement of the parties, CEDR will nominate independent third parties as mediators and the latter after a consultation with the parties will usually attend meetings, where appropriate, chair and determine procedure for mediation, assist the parties in drawing up any written agreement and abide by the terms of the Model Procedure, the Mediation Agreement and CEDR's Code of Conduct. The parties are required to accept that in relation to a dispute neither the mediator nor CEDR use an agent or act in any capacity for any of the parties. The mediator must act as an independent contractor and as an agent or employee of CEDR.

CEDR, in conjunction with the mediator, makes the necessary arrangements for the mediation, including the nomination of the mediator to organise a suitable venue and dates, exchange of the summaries and documents, meeting with any or all representatives if the mediator has been appointed and general administration of mediation. The mediation agreement is drawn up by the mediator in agreement with the parties.

As to the procedure, each participant states in the mediation agreement the names of the persons who represent their cases and also any other person who may be participating in the mediation. Each party is required to send to CEDR at least two weeks before the mediation or such other date as may be agreed between the parties and CEDR sufficient copies of the summary of its case and the documents on which it relies. CEDR ensures that documents have been exchanged between the parties. The mediation takes place at the place and time stated in the mediation agreement and it is for the mediator to determine the procedure of the mediation. No formal record or transcript of the mediation is made. In the event of the parties being unable to reach a settlement, with the consent of the representatives the mediator produces for the parties a non-binding recommendation on the terms of settlement. However, in order for a settlement to be legally binding it must be in writing and signed on behalf of the parties.

Under the CEDR rules it is possible for a party to withdraw from the mediation at any time and the mediator will, in writing, inform their representatives. But, of course, any mediation will terminate where any of the following has taken place:

(a) a party has withdrawn from the mediation; or

(b) a written settlement is concluded; or

(c) the mediator has decided that to continue mediation is unlikely; or

(d) the mediator has decided that he should retire for any of the reasons in the Code of Conduct.

Under CEDR Rules it is possible for the parties to be engaged in litigation or arbitration in relation to the dispute on which mediation also has been commenced unless the parties agree otherwise.

Confidentiality is an important issue in mediation; CEDR Mediation Procedure and Agreement provide that every person involved in the mediation would keep all information confidential and must not use them for any collateral or ulterior purpose. Information disclosed at the mediation will be without prejudice, privileged and inadmissible as evidence or subject to discovery in any litigation or arbitration relating to the dispute.

None of the parties to the mediation agreement is entitled to call the mediator or CEDR or any of its employees, consultants, officers or representatives as a witness or an expert or an arbitrator in any litigation or arbitration in relation to the dispute.

CEDR fees, including fees of the mediator and other expenses of mediation, must be borne equally by the parties. The exclusion of a liability clause is important and it provides that neither the mediator nor CEDR shall be liable to the parties for any act or omission in connection with the mediation unless the act or omission is shown to have been in bad faith.

CEDR ensures that the procedure for mediation is flexible in order to adapt it to suit the parties. CEDR Rules may be applied to domestic and international disputes as well as to multi-party disputes.

In the event of CEDR being asked by a party to initiate a mediation it will approach the other party or parties to a dispute to persuade them to participate. Alternatively, the party which has taken the initiative to propose mediation may send a draft agreement based on the Model Agreement to the other party. CEDR recognises that the success of mediation depends to a considerable extent on the skill of the mediator, its rules of procedure provide for more than one mediator or independent expert, where necessary.

The Model ADR Contract Clauses primarily provide for a fast-track drafting guide to the key ADR clauses and model contract clauses for negotiation, mediation and executive tribunal[13]. As stated earlier, it is for the parties to decide whether they will accept the CEDR Model ADR Contract Clauses. CEDR, however, prefers that court proceedings or arbitration in relation to a dispute should not ideally be commenced until the mediation process has been exhausted although it maintains that commencement of mediation should not prevent the parties from initiating or continuing with court proceedings.

In accordance with the acknowledged theme of ADR, CEDR also believes that participants should take an active role in mediating their disputes or differences, and that a mediator should ideally play a facilitative role, unless the mediation process has reached a deadlock. In order that his neutrality may not be questioned by any party, CEDR maintains that a mediator's recommendations will be without prejudice and will not be binding.

The Model ADR Contract Clauses developed by CEDR is open to parties; there is no need to explain the provisions in this document because if the parties wish to be governed by CEDR procedure, they will automatically consult this document.

10.4 LONDON COURT OF INTERNATIONAL ARBITRATION ("LCIA")

10.4.1 Introduction – A Discussion of the Main Provisions of the LCIA Mediation Procedure

LCIA mediation may be activated where an agreement provides for mediation under the procedure of Rules of the LCIA as the assumption is that the parties have agreed to be governed by the LCIA procedures and Rules. The LCIA mediation procedure includes the Schedule of Mediation Fees and Expenses which may be amended from time to time by the LCIA court. It is the purpose of this section to briefly discuss the mediation procedures under the LCIA Rules which deal with the following:

(a) commencing mediation where prior agreement to mediate exists;

(b) commencing mediation where no prior agreement to mediate exists;

(c) appointment of mediators;

(d) statement by the parties;

[13] An Executive Tribunal is also known as a mini-trial, which entails a more structured opening presentations addressed to a panel comprising a senior executive for each party and a neutral individual.

(e) conduct of the mediation;

(f) settlement agreement;

(g) costs;

(h) judicial or arbitral proceedings;

(i) confidentiality and privacy;

(j) exclusion of liability; and

(k) schedule of mediation fees and expenses.

These items are now discussed briefly.

10.4.1.1 Commencing Mediation where an Agreement to Mediate Exists

Where a contract has provided for mediation under the LCIA Rules, if the parties should wish to commence mediation, they are required to send to the Registrar of the LCIA a written request for mediation briefly stating therein the nature of the dispute and the value of the claim. This request must also be accompanied by a copy of a prior agreement, the names, addresses and contact numbers of the parties to the mediation and of their legal representatives, if known, and of the name of the mediator, if already nominated. Where the Request for Mediation is not made jointly by all parties to the prior agreement, the party commencing the mediation must send a copy of the Request for Mediation to the other party or parties. The Request for Mediation shall be accompanied by the registration fee prescribed in the Schedule. If a mediator has not been proposed by the party or parties, the LCIA court shall appoint a mediator as soon as possible after receipt by the Registrar of the Request for Mediation. In appointing a mediator regard shall be had to the nature of the dispute and issues involved in it. Where there is a prior agreement, the date of commencement of the mediation shall be the date of receipt by the Registrar of the Request for Mediation.

10.4.1.2 Commencement of Mediation where no Prior Agreement Exists

Where no prior agreement as to mediation exists a party may request mediation under the LCIA procedure and send that request to the Registrar stating briefly the nature of a dispute, the value of the claim, in addition to giving names and addresses of the parties, their legal representatives, if known, and of the proposed or nominated mediator, if any. The Request for Mediation shall be accompanied by the registration fee. Where a Request for Mediation is not made by all the parties concerned, the party wishing to commence mediation shall send a copy of a Request for Mediation to all parties. The other party or parties shall within 14 days of receiving the Request for Mediation advise the Registrar, in writing, whether or not they would be prepared to come to mediation. If the other parties decline the invitation then there is no need to initiate mediation; however, where mediation is accepted by all parties concerned, the LCIA court shall appoint a mediator as soon as practicable with due regard for any method or criteria of selection or nomination agreed in writing by the parties. But all appointments must be made having regard to the issue of costs (Article 8 of the Procedure). Where there does not exist any prior agreement the date of commencement of mediation shall be the date on which the agreement to mediate is reached.

10.4.1.3 Appointment of the Mediator

Appointments of mediators by the LCIA court are primarily based on past and present professional positions, and where a nomination has been made by the parties themselves the court will pay attention to that and the method or criteria of selection agreed in writing by the parties in addition to paying attention to the issue of costs. However, in order to maintain his or her neutrality, after selection, he or she must sign a declaration to the effect that there are no circumstances known to him or her which would give rise to any justifiable doubts as to his or her impartiality or independence. Where the mediator has not been nominated by the parties themselves a copy of his résumé and declaration shall be provided to the parties. A party retains its right to object to a mediator's appointment on the grounds of justified doubts as to his or her impartiality or independence. Where a mediator's appointment is rejected the LCIA court shall appoint a mediator.

10.4.1.4 Statement by the Parties

It is for the parties to agree how and in what form they will inform the mediator of their respective cases and in usual circumstances each party is required to submit to the mediator a brief statement summarising his case and the issues to be resolved no later than 7 days before the date agreed between the mediator and the parties for the first scheduled mediation session.

Each witness statement should be accompanied by documentary evidence, where necessary, and each party is required to submit a copy of his written statement and supporting documents to the other party or parties.

10.4.1.5 Conduct of Mediation and Settlement Agreement

Articles 5 and 6 are respectively concerned with the conduct and conclusion of mediation. Under the LCIA Rules, the manner in which a mediation may be conducted and may be determined is in the light of the circumstances of the case and the wishes of the parties. Thus, his/her discretionary power is subject to the choice of the parties and the circumstances of each case. During the conduct of a mediation, a mediator may communicate with the parties either orally or in writing, and may convene meetings at venue(s) to be determined by the mediator in consultation with the parties. The contents of any private discussion with a party must not be communicated to the other party without the consent of the party making the communication. It is for each party to notify the other party and the mediator of the identity of the individuals who will attend any meeting that may be convened by the mediator. Unless otherwise agreed by the parties, the mediator decides on the language(s) of the mediation.

Under the LCIA Rule, the parties very much have the choice as to how their mediation may be conducted.

A mediation will come to an end in any of the following circumstances:

(a) a settlement agreement has been signed by the parties; or

(b) the parties believe that no settlement may be reached, and therefore they would wish to terminate the mediation; or

(c) according to the mediator, the mediation process will not resolve the issues in dispute; or

(d) the time limit indicated in a Prior Agreement has expired and that the parties have not extended that time limit.

Initiative to draft the settlement agreement should be taken by the parties themselves, and the mediator will provide assistance in this regard, if so requested by the parties. The LCIA Rules maintain that by signing a settlement agreement, the parties give their consent to be bound by it.

10.4.1.6 Costs

Costs of mediations under the LCIA Procedure entail the fees and expenses of the mediator, administrative charges of the LCIA, and any other costs incurred by the parties, e.g. experts' fees or any other related expenses. Unless otherwise agreed by them, the costs are to be borne equally by the parties. No mediator will be appointed unless a deposit determined by the LCIA, in equal shares has been paid by the parties. The total costs are determined after the mediation has been concluded, or upon abandonment. If the costs exceed the deposit, the shortfall must be paid by the parties in equal shares; where however the deposit exceeds the costs, the excess is reimbursed to the parties proportionally.

10.4.1.7 Confidentiality and Privacy

All mediation sessions are held in private, and all statements and documents for the purpose of the mediation are confidential in nature and delivered on a "*without prejudice*" basis, and are to be regarded as "*privileged*" documents. By the same token, all discussion and terms of settlement shall remain confidential, and neither the mediator nor the parties shall disclose any information pertaining to one party to another.

All documents and/or information used or produced during the mediation shall remain privileged and will not be treated as admissible evidence nor may be used in any litigation or arbitration except for any document or information which would in any event be admissible or disclosable. This is because privacy and confidentiality are the two most important factors which seem to attract people to mediation.

10.4.1.8 Other Issues

Under the LCIA Rules, unless the parties have agreed otherwise, the parties, despite initiating mediation, may institute court or arbitral proceedings or continue with an existing mediation, on the same issues under dispute.

Again, under the LCIA Rules, neither the LCIA, nor the LCIA court, including their members, employees and any mediator shall be liable to any party howsoever for any act or omission in connection with the conduct of any mediation unless a particular wrongful act or omission was committed consciously and deliberately by any of its members and the mediator.

By the same token, neither the LCIA nor LCIA court, including their members and employees, is under any legal obligation to make any statement to any person in connection with the mediation, nor shall any person seek to make any of these person a witness in any proceedings, legal or otherwise, arising out of the mediation.

LCIA has also developed model clauses in regard to mediation.

10.5 RULES OF THE MEDIATION INSTITUTE OF THE STOCKHOLM CHAMBER OF COMMERCE

These Rules were adopted by the Stockholm Chamber of Commerce and came into force on 1 April 1999. The Mediation Institute of the Stockholm Chamber of Commerce is part of the Arbitration Institute of the Stockholm Chamber of Commerce. Two alternative features of these Rules, amongst others, stand out:

(a) that unless otherwise agreed by the parties, the time limit for mediation is two months; and

(b) that after reaching a settlement agreement, the parties have the choice of appointing the mediator as an arbitrator to confirm the settlement agreement in the form of an arbitral award.

The Mediation Rules of the Stockholm Chamber of Commerce Mediation Institute are now briefly described. Article 1 of the Rules provides that a mediator must be impartial and independent and that unless otherwise agreed by the parties, a mediator may not act as an arbitrator in any future arbitration pertaining to the subject matter of the dispute. In order to maintain his/her neutrality, prior to his accepting the appointment as a mediator, he/she must disclose any circumstances which might give rise to doubts as his/her impartiality and independence. Furthermore, even after his/her appointment if he/she becomes aware of any circumstances which might render him/her ineligible for acting as a mediator, he must immediately inform the parties, in writing, accordingly, and presumably the Mediation Institute of the Stockholm Chamber of Commerce.

Unless otherwise agreed by the parties, the mediator, the Mediation Institute of the Stockholm Chamber of Commerce, the parties and any other individual who may be participating in mediation, must maintain confidentiality in all respects. Should a party so request, all documents and other material provided in the course of a mediation must be returned to that party, without retaining any copy thereof; by the same token, should a party so request, any notes taken in the course of a mediation shall be destroyed as soon as the mediation terminates. Any views expressed or any statement made by a party in the course of a mediation may not be introduced as evidence in any proceedings, judicial or arbitral, nor may it be required to be involved in any such proceedings as a witness. This policy also applies to mediators and experts who have been involved in the relevant mediation process.

Mediation may be initiated either by a party or all parties concerned jointly; however the Request for Mediation must be submitted to the Mediation Institute of the Stockholm Chamber of Commerce in writing including the names, addresses, contact numbers of the parties and Counsels, summary of the dispute and the statement confirming whether parties have agreed to mediate a dispute. In the event of a Request for Mediation being submitted by one party only the Institute shall communicate the request to the other party; the other party must notify the Institute of whether it would participate in the mediation. All requests for mediation must be registered on paying a fee.

Unless otherwise agreed by the parties, the Mediation Institute shall appoint a sole mediator but before the appointment is made the Mediation Institute shall seek the views of the parties. Where the parties nominate a person as a mediator that person shall be appointed by the Mediation Institute. In the absence of any agreement between the parties to the contrary, where more than one mediator needs to be appointed each party shall appoint equal number of mediators, and if an odd number of mediators is to be appointed the Mediation Institute shall appoint a mediator who shall act as a chairman. If a mediator is prevented from fulfilling his duties or fails to perform his functions in an adequate manner then the Institute shall remove the mediator and replace him/her as soon as possible but before so doing the Institute must seek the views of the parties and of the mediator.

Unless otherwise agreed by the parties, each party is required to contribute half of the advance on costs, which would be determined by the Mediation Institute. However, there is no objection to any of the parties settling the entire costs, although sharing of the expenditure by the parties concerned is the common phenomenon. The final amount of costs is determined by the Mediation Institute. If a party should fail to pay any amount of the costs so determined (the Advance on Costs), the dispute shall be dismissed either wholly or in part proportionate to the missing payment. Under these Rules, the

Mediation Costs consist of: (a) the Mediatior's fee; (b) administrative fee of the Mediation Institute of the Stockholm Chamber of Commerce; and (c) any other expenses incurred during the course of a mediation.

In compliance with the wishes of the parties the mediator is required to determine the conduct of the mediation and the rules of natural justice, that is, neutrality of the mediator and the *audi alteram partem* rule must be observed. Should however the mediator believe that the dispute is not likely to be resolved through mediation, he may suggest other means of resolving it; it is not clear what other means of resolving disputes might be suggested by the mediator.

Unless otherwise agreed by the parties, the mediation shall terminate within two months of the date when the dispute was first referred to the mediator; in other words, two months is the usual time limit for settling the dispute, however, at the request of the mediator the Institute may extend this time.

The mediation shall terminate in any of the following circumstances:

(a) by concluding a settlement agreement between the parties;

(b) by a declaration of the mediator and the Mediation Institute to the effect that mediation is unlikely to lead to the settlement of a dispute; or

(c) by a written request by a party to the mediator that mediation should be terminated.

Under the Rules it is possible for the parties, after achieving a settlement agreement to agree to appoint a mediator as an arbitrator and request him/her to confirm the settlement agreement in an arbitral award (Article 12).

The parties remain jointly and severally liable for all payments and usually they bear the mediation costs in equal shares.

The Mediation Rules of the Stockholm Chamber of Commerce Mediation Institute contain many important elements which may be found in the Rules of other Institutions such as the ICC or CEDR. However, one of the attributes of the Mediation Rules of the Stockholm Chamber of Commerce Mediation Institute is that an agreement reached through a mediation process may be transformed into an arbitral award.

10.6 INTERNATIONAL CENTRE FOR SETTLEMENT OF INVESTMENT DISPUTES (ICSID)

10.6.1 ICSID Conciliation Rules

The systems of settling disputes by conciliation or by judicial means (arbitration) were developed by the Convention on Settlement of Investment Disputes between States and Nationals of Other States, 1965, which Convention came into force in 1966. It was one of the early international conventions during the post second war era which promoted the idea of settling investment disputes, primarily emanating from State contracts, by means of conciliation and/or arbitration. Parties to these disputes are usually a State and a transnational corporation (a private foreign investor). In order for a dispute to be referred to a Conciliation Commission or a tribunal, both the State party and the State in which the transnational corporation is registered / incorporated must be parties to the ICSID Convention on an ad hoc basis; furthermore, the dispute must be regarded as an *"investment"* dispute. The Convention has not defined an *"investment dispute"*, but the general meaning of the term, in the context of a dispute is usually applied. The meaning of *"investment"* must be understood by referring to the spirit of the Convention[14].

Although the Convention provides for two distinctly identifiable methods of settling investment disputes, conciliation and arbitration, it is not necessary for a party to a dispute to exhaust both methods; in other words, a party has the right to refer its dispute to an ICSID tribunal, without going through an ICSID Conciliation Commission.

It is to be pointed out however that the ICSID Convention did not refer to mediation as a method of setting investment disputes coming under its purview; instead it provided for conciliation. Settlement of disputes by ADR methods includes conciliation too; thus, it has been decided to discuss the ICSID Conciliation system in the context of this work.

Under the ICSID Convention, conciliations should be achieved with the assistance of experts; hence it provided for panels of experts, and for each dispute a separate conciliation commission is set up bearing in mind the nature of the dispute.

Each Contracting State may designate four persons for the Conciliation panels. Article 14(1) of the Convention provides that:

> *"Persons designated to serve on the Panels shall be persons of high moral character and recognized competence in the fields of law, commerce, industry or finance, who may be relied upon to exercise independent judgment. "*

Each Panel member serves for a renewable period of six years.

All requests for conciliation must be addressed to the Secretary-General, in writing, who sends a copy of the request to the other party. A request for conciliation will not be registered if, according to the Secretary-General, the dispute is manifestly outside the jurisdiction of the Centre[15].

A Commission may consist of a sole conciliator or any uneven number of conciliators as the parties may agree. In the event of the parties failing to agree upon the number of conciliators, and the method of their appointment, a commission consists of three conciliators; one conciliator to be appointed by

---

[14] See ICSID, *Documents concerning the Origin and the Foundation of the Convention*, 1968, vol. II at 702, 704, 707, 826, 844, 972; see further C Chatterjee, "Investment-related Promissory Notes are Investments under the ICSID Convention: *Fedax NV v The Republic of Venezuela*, 3 *Journal of World Investment*, (2002) 147-159

[15] Article 28(1)

each party, and the third by agreement of the parties. If a Commission is not constituted within 90 days after registration of the request, the Secretary-General at the request of either party and after consulting both parties may appoint the conciliator or conciliators not yet appointed.

Conciliators may be appointed from outside the Panel of Conciliators, but such conciliators shall possess the qualities and qualifications applicable to those of the conciliators who are appointed from the Panel of Conciliators.

The Commission is the judge of its own competence[16]. All conciliation proceedings are conducted in accordance with the Conciliation Rules[17]. Conciliation Commissions clarify the issues in dispute between the parties and endeavour to bring about agreement between the parties on mutually acceptable terms. A Conciliation Commission recommends to the parties settlement of their dispute at any stage of proceedings.

If the parties reach an agreement, the Commission draws up a report, stating the issues in dispute and confirming that the parties have reached an agreement. However, if it should appear to the Commission that there is no prospect of the parties reaching any agreement, it closes the proceedings and draws up a report accordingly. Neither party shall invoke or rely on any views expressed or statements or admissions or offers of settlement made by the other party in a conciliation proceedings or any recommendation made by the Commission in any other proceedings.

The ICSID Conciliation Rules have been developed in the following Chapters:

Chapter I Establishment of the Commission (Rules 1-12)

Chapter II Working of the Commission (Rules 13-18)

Chapter III General Procedural Provisions (Rules 19–21)

Chapter IV Conciliation Procedures (Rules 22-28)

Chapter V Termination of the Proceeding (Rules 29-33)

Chapter VI Final Provisions (Rule 34)

The basic contents of these Chapters are now being discussed.

10.6.1.1 Establishment of the Commission

In order to initiate a conciliation proceeding the aggrieved party is required to submit to the Registrar's office a request for conciliation. Requests for conciliation are registered only if they have sufficient merits. Upon notification of the registration of the request for conciliation, the parties are required to constitute a Commission, and it is primarily for them to agree on the number of conciliators and the method of their appointment. However, in the absence

---

[16] Article 32

[17] These Rules are discussed below.

of any previous agreement between the parties as to the number of conciliators, and the method of their appointment, the following procedure may apply:

(i) the requesting party shall, within 10 days after the registration of the request, propose to the other party the appointment of a sole conciliator or of a specified even number of conciliators are the method of their appointment must also be specified;

(ii) within 20 days after receipt of the requesting party's proposal, the requested party shall either accept the proposal or make its own proposal; and

(iii) within 20 days after receipt of the reply, the requesting party shall notify the requested party of its acceptance or rejection of the proposal.

The parties are required to promptly notify the Secretary-General of ICSID whether they have reached any agreement on the appointment of a conciliator or conciliators. Should however it be found that 60 days after the registration of a request, no agreement on another procedure has been reached by the parties themselves, then the Commission is to be constituted in accordance with the formula provided for in Article 29(2)(b) of the Convention, and the Secretary-General must be informed accordingly. Article 29(2)(b) provides that:

> *"Where the parties do not agree upon the number of conciliators and the method of their appointment, the Commission shall consist of three conciliators, one conciliator appointed by each party and the third, who shall be the president of the Commission, appointed by agreement of the parties."*

In the event of the Commission not being constituted within 90 days after the notice of registration has been despatched by the Secretary-General, or such other period as the parties may agree, either party may, through the Secretary-General request the Chairman of the Administrative Council, in writing, appoint a conciliator to be the President of the Commission. These appointments will be made within 30 days of the date on which such a request is made[18], and the Secretary-General shall notify the parties of any appointment or designation made by the Chairman of the Administrative Council.

It is for the party or parties concerned to notify the Secretary-General of the appointment of each conciliator, and the latter or the Chairman of the Administrative Council seeks an acceptance from the appointee[19]. In the event of a conciliator failing to accept his appointment within 15 days, the Secretary-General promptly notifies the parties, and, if appropriate, the Chairman, and

[18] Rule 4 of the Rules of Procedure for Conciliation (Conciliation Rules).

[19] Rule 5 of the Conciliation Rules, op. cit.,

asks them to arrange for the appointment of another conciliator in accordance with the method followed in respect of the previous appointment.

A Conciliation Commission is deemed to be constituted and the proceedings to have begun on the date on which the Secretary-General notifies the parties that all the conciliators have accepted their appointment. Conciliators are also required to declare that they shall not accept any instruction or compensation with regard to the proceedings from any source other than those provided in the ICSID Convention.

Replacement of a Conciliator may be made by common consent of the parties to a dispute and a conciliator may submit his/her resignation to the other members of the Commission and the Secretary-General of ICSID on the grounds of his/her duties. The Commission may accept his/her resignation after consideration and notify the party concerned, if he/she was appointed by that party, and the Secretary-General. It is possible for a party to a dispute to propose the disqualification of a Conciliator pursuant to Article 57 of the Convention[20], but such proposal shall be made before the Commission recommends the terms of settlement of the dispute to the parties or at the closure of the proceedings (whichever is earlier). A disqualification proposal, supported by reason, is filed with the Secretary-General, who transmits it to the members of the Commission. The Conciliator concerned must without delay, submit explanations to the Commission or the Chairman, as the case may be[21]. Unless the proposal relates to a majority of the members of a Commission, the other members, in the absence of the Conciliator concerned, promptly consider the proposal, and if these members are equally divided, they notify the Chairman of the explanation submitted by the Conciliator concerned and of their failure to reach a decision. All communications must be sent through the Secretary-General of ICSID. The Chairman is required to take a decision on such issues within 30 days of the receipt of the proposal by him. Incidentally, the proceedings are suspended until a decision has been taken on the proposal.

In the event of a vacancy arising on the Commission, the Secretary-General is required to notify forthwith the parties, the Chairman of the Administrative Council, if necessary, of the disqualification, death, incapacity or resignation of a conciliator. With the appointment of a new conciliator, the Commission may hold the hearing afresh, in whole, or in part.

10.6.1.2 Working of the Commission

The Commission holds its first session within 60 days after a tribunal has been constituted, or such other period as the parties may agree. Conciliation

---

[20] Article 57 provides that: *"A party may propose to a Commission or Tribunal the disqualification of any of its members on account of any fact indicating a manifest lack of the qualities required by paragraph (1) of Article 14. A party to arbitration proceedings may, in addition, propose the disqualification of an arbitrator on the ground that he was ineligible for appointment to the Tribunal under Section 2 of Chapter IV."*

[21] Rule 9(3)

Commissions usually meet at the seat of the Centre or at such other place as may have been agreed between the parties. Choice of the venue other than the Centre, must be consulted with the Secretary-General of ICSID and approved by the Conciliation Commission.

The President of the Commission conducts its hearings and presides at its deliberations. These deliberations take place in private and remain confidential. Usually, only members of the Commission take part in the deliberations of the Commission.

Commissions take their decisions by majority votes. The Rules permit Commission to take their decisions by correspondence among its members. Decisions taken by such method are certified by the President of the Commission.

Each party may be represented or assisted by agents, counsels or advocates.

10.6.1.3 General Procedural Provisions

Conciliation Commissions make orders for the conduct of proceedings. In regard to preliminary procedural consultation however the parties' views are sought by the President, particularly in respect of the following: the number of members of a Commission required to constitute a quorum at its sittings; the language(s) of the proceedings, the nature of evidence whether oral or written each party intends to produce, the time limit by which such evidence should be produced; and the manner in which the record of the hearings shall be preserved. But, of course, in the conduct of proceedings, Commissions apply agreements, if any, between the parties on procedural matters.

10.6.1.4 Conciliation Procedures and the Functions of Commissions

Conciliation Commissions attempt to bring about agreement between the parties from time to time at any stage of proceedings by making recommendations to the parties. A Conciliation Commission may recommend that:

> "*. . . the parties accept specific terms of settlement or that they refrain, while it seeks to bring about agreement between them, from specific acts that might aggravate the dispute; it shall point out to the parties the arguments in favor of its recommendations.*"[22]

A Commission may request from either party oral explanations, documents and any other information, including evidence from other persons, and with consent of the party concerned, visit the location of an incident, if necessary.

The parties are expected to co-operate, in good faith, with a Commission, and furnish all relevant documents, information and explanations, and to

[22] Rule 22 of the *Rules of Procedure for Conciliation,* op. cit.

facilitate visits to and inquiries at any location connected with the dispute; if that Commission deems such visits necessary[23].

As soon as the Commission is constituted, the Secretary-General transmits to each member a copy of the request by means of which the proceeding was initiated, along with the supporting documentation and any communication received from either party[24].

Written statements are required to be submitted within 30 days or such longer time as the President of the Commission or, in the absence of the President, the Secretary-General deems.

The hearings of the Commission take place in private and remain confidential. With the consent of the parties, the Commission decides which other persons besides the parties, their agents, counsels and advocates, witnesses and experts may attend the hearings. The Commission may hear the witnesses and experts whose evidence a party may consider relevant[25].

10.6.1.5 Termination of the Proceeding

Challenges to the jurisdiction of the Centre are to be made as soon as possible. In fact, objections to jurisdiction should ideally be submitted to the Secretary-General no later than when the first written statement is submitted or at the first hearing, whichever is earlier, unless the facts on which the objection is based are unknown to that party at that time[26].

On its own initiative, the Conciliation Commission may, at any stage of the proceeding, consider whether the dispute is within the jurisdiction of the Centre. While considering the issue of jurisdiction, the proceeding on the merits shall be suspended. The Commission considers the views of the parties on the objection. The Commission deals with the objection as a preliminary question or joins it to the merits of the dispute. Where the Commission overrules the objection or joins it to the merits, it considers the latter without delay. In the event of the Commission deciding that the dispute is beyond the jurisdiction of the Centre, or not within its competence, it closes the proceeding and draws up a reasoned report to that effect.

The Commission closes proceedings and draws up its report if the parties reach an agreement on the issues in dispute. On the other hand, if at any stage of the proceedings it should appear to the Commission that there is no likelihood of any agreement between the parties, it, after notifying the parties, closes the proceedings and draws up its report in writing accordingly, within a maximum period of 30 days from the closure of the proceedings.

---

[23] Rule 23 of the *Rules of Procedure for Conciliation*, op. cit.,

[24] Rule 24

[25] Rule 28(1)

[26] Rule 29

10.7 SOCIOLOGICAL AND POLITICAL ELEMENTS OF A DISPUTE

At the outset, it must be pointed out that the term *"dispute"* must not be misused; for lawyers it has a definite meaning, that is, whether a dispute is a justiciable (legal) or non-justiciable (non-legal) dispute. It is elementary that a dispute may be a mixed dispute, that is, it may contain both legal and non-legal issues, but on balance, when a dispute contains a sufficient number of legal issues which merit a judicial consideration for providing remedies to a party, it is then usually regarded as a justiciable dispute[27].

Purely non-legal disputes should be regarded as differences, although many lawyers may find this distinction between *"disputes"* and *"differences"* rather controversial, but certainly lawyers trained in public international law generally maintain this distinction.

Disputes usually arise for two reasons: (a) when parties maintain that two different interpretations may be given to a contractual provision or a provision of a statute or a treaty, and (b) when differences become manifest as to the understanding of provisions and the assumptions on which provisions are based. Differences of understanding of provisions may be settled without taking a legalistic approach and this is where perhaps alternative dispute resolution method becomes most relevant; however, it may be unjust to settle disputes of a legal nature solely by non-legal methods.

It must be noted however that differences may lead to a dispute; therefore it would be advisable to settle the difference, when possible, by applying non-judicial or non-legal methods. For instance, disputes of a matrimonial nature or industrial disputes can be largely non-legal and therefore in most instances may be settled by non-legal methods, and once parties have reached an agreement it may be legitimised by legal means so that a breach of the agreed settlement may be remedied by judicial means. In many cases, political disputes represent political differences for achieving political gains. An acquisition of title to a territory, for example, may in many ways be described as a political gain although justification for the title to a territory may have to be confirmed by legal and historical evidence. Abundant examples are available to establish that boundary disputes, whether bilateral or multilateral, have been settled by conciliation commissions or by arbitrators.

The establishment of Advisory, Conciliation and Arbitration Service ("ACAS") in the United Kingdom signifies that not all so-called employment disputes require legal consideration; they are occasioned by different views maintained by employers and employees on certain procedural issues or compulsory statutory issues. When an employment dispute is referred to ACAS it really is not to be treated as a fully justiciable dispute. ACAS' services may be regarded as an alternative dispute resolution method of settling disputes.

---

[27] See further C Chatterjee, *Fedax v The Republic of Venezuela*, op. cit.

The term *"conflict"* seems to be over-used by many, be they lawyers or non-lawyers, although the term often appears in international relations, in the final analysis what is conflict is primarily a difference of opinion based on each party's perception of rights and claims. From this standpoint, all differences are, to a certain extent, based on psychological perceptions of parties. Sociological aspects of *"any difference"* is also based on different perceptions of different social groups whose aspirations may have to be taken into account by a government in developing legislation, but commercial disputes may not necessarily make any room for such aspirations. Sociological elements of a dispute are therefore philosophically orientated, perception-based and remote from offering any aid to resolving an actual dispute, particularly of a commercial nature. When dispute settlement is to be achieved by referring to legislative provisions, or provisions of a contract or a treaty, sociological aspirations of social groups may have to be disregarded, but, of course, where law or treaty provisions prove to be inadequate to deal with a particular situation requiring a determination of rights and remedies of a party, judicial institutions have, in certain cases, relied upon what is known as the teleological approach to law. In the *Anglo-Norwegian Fisheries'* case,[28] despite derogations from customary rules of international law by Norway, derogations which were accepted by the International Court of Justice on the grounds of estoppel, the Court paid attention to the economic realities in that for Norway fisheries are one of the most important sources of income, special consideration in regard to delimitation of the territorial sea would not be inappropriate. This may be interpreted as a teleological approach to law.

A sociological approach to resolving differences, whether between a social group or a government or between two parties, must be regarded as an extra-legislative approach which may not necessarily create precedents. Sociological approach to settling disputes therefore is based on an ad hoc approach to settlement of disputes. The primary purpose of settling a dispute or difference is to provide remedies to individuals and/or social groups and to acknowledge their rights. From this standpoint there is no need to adopt any totally legalistic or judicial method of settling disputes provided non-judicial methods do not derogate from any legal rules.

10.8 CONCLUSIONS

Institutional mediations are conducted according to the Rules of the institution concerned. Common elements in these Rules are available. Depending upon the subject matter of mediation, the nature of evidence may vary. Although a number of mediation institutions are available, the basic theme of mediation remains the same – a solution of a dispute or difference on agreed terms.

Although mediation has a relatively long history, the qualities that a mediator should possess still remain undefined. There seems to exist a perception

[28] ICJ Reports (1951) 116

that a highly qualified person, with experience and training would make a successful mediator; but the issue of the understanding of the cultures, in the case of international mediations, or where a party or parties hail from two different cultures, remains. A mediator in many respects resembles a negotiator of contracts. The nature of the issues may have to be related to cultures and the party's understanding of the problems and issues.

A mediator must be able to understand the oral statements made by the parties; this becomes particularly important when the parties express themselves in a foreign language. A responsible mediator must be prepared to understand what the parties mean to say. Patience and tolerance prove to be virtues of a good mediator.

A mediator must be unbiased and knowledgeable so that the parties place trust in him/her. He/she must also create confidence in the minds of the parties to a mediation. He/she must demonstrate his/her understanding of the matter/issues in dispute. Neutrality in all respects must be shown by him/her in conducting mediation sessions. Culture-based disputes should be mediated by mediators who have a thorough knowledge of the cultures concerned, and technical disputes must be mediated by those who have expert knowledge in the subject matter of the dispute.

CHAPTER 11

Enforcement Issues

11.1 INTRODUCTION

The ADR system of dispute settlement is informal in nature and attempts are made to ensure that no court procedure or court environment is applied and developed. There is thus the perception that ADR-based results would not be binding.

If two parties agree to settle their dispute by an ADR process, and reach an agreement based on their mutual consent, then the mutually agreed terms, when drafted, become contractual terms and there is no reason why from a legal standpoint any of these terms, if in breach, may not entitle a party to enforce the agreement. The agreement is as good as a simple contract and therefore the instrument must be subject to the law of contract of the place at which ADR takes place.

However, over the years the enforcement procedures for ADR processes have been developed in two forms: adjudicatory and non-adjudicatory. Settlements reached in a non-adjudicatory process may be transformed into consent judgements. It is the purpose of this chapter to discuss the issue of enforcement of ADR-based agreements and how these agreements may be enforced.

11.2 AN EXAMINATION OF THE LEGAL STATUS OF AGREEMENTS REACHED BY PARTIES THROUGH ADR PROCESSES

If parties agree to the terms of settlement, the intention to accept these terms becomes manifest; in other words, the intention to be bound by these terms will have the effect of a contractual agreement. The legal status of such agreements would be considered by the courts by referring to judicial guidelines developed by them in relation to the intention to create legal relations. There is no need to go into details of all the cases pertaining to this topic in the law of contract but for the sake of establishing the main theme of this chapter, it is thought appropriate to refer to some of those decisions rendered by the English courts. The question which must be raised in this connection is that if there was no intention to settle a dispute, why should the parties agree to draft the terms of their settlement? What should also be considered is whether the effect of ADR is being undermined by referring to the issue of enforceability rather than to the contractual effect of those agreements.

A contractual agreement under English law is usually based on the intention of parties to create legal relations between them; the principle of *ad idem* should apply and, once the mutual consent becomes available, there is no reason why the legal effect of such consent might not be affirmed.

11.3 THE INTENTION TO ENFORCE WHEN REACHING A SETTLEMENT

All ADR based settlements are consensual, thus there is no reason to believe that the intention to create legal relations did not exist in reaching a settlement. Upon signature of the agreed settlement by the parties concerned, the status of a simple contract is attained; the issue of consideration does not arise, when one looks for reason of reaching a settlement, the settlement is, in fact, a judgement; the only difference being that it is reached by the parties themselves under the ADR mechanism and without the assistance of a court. The whole ADR mechanism will fail if this issue of mutual settlement having the force of a judgement is not appropriately conceived.

As to the intention to create legal relations, there is no need to go into details of the principles of the law of contract; it is opportune however to make references to some of the decisions of the Courts in certain important cases pertaining to intention to create legal relations into the law of contract.

In both *Channel Tunnel Group Ltd & Another v Balfour Beatty Construction Ltd & Others*[1] and *Cott UK Ltd v F E Barber Ltd*[2] it was acknowledged by the courts that where the parties have chosen an alternative method of settling their disputes there is reason why a stay of proceedings by a court of law may not be allowed. In the *Cott* case Hegarthy J stated that:

> *"... even where there is no arbitration clause, in the light of the observations of Lord Mustill in the Channel Tunnel Group case, and in the light of the changing attitudes of a legal system, the court plainly has a jurisdiction to stay under its inherent jurisdiction, where the parties have chosen some alternative means of dispute resolution."*[3]

11.4 A DISCUSSION OF THE ADJUDICATORY AND NON-ADJUDICATORY PROCESSES

An agreement reached during court proceedings has the force of a decision or judgment, and in the event of a breach, the aggrieved party may enforce it. A non-adjudicatory process does not involve a third party determination of the issues; it is based on the consensual agreement between the parties and therefore the form of such agreement will also be determined by the parties

[1] [1993] 1 All ER at 664

[2] [1997] 3 All ER at 540

[3] op. cit., at 548

themselves. Agreements reached by and through non-adjudicatory process may or may not be enforced as in some situations the parties themselves may not plan any enforcement. Through a non-adjudicatory process they would perhaps like to know their legal position, and, having become aware of their position, will behave themselves accordingly. In other words, in a non-adjudicatory process the issue of enforcement may not be the prime issue and hence the question of enforcing the agreements reached by such a process may not necessarily arise. It is quite possible however for the parties to convert a non-binding settlement into a binding one and thus accord enforceability under the law of contract. In the United States a court-annexed ADR process thus becomes enforceable as it is genuinely regulated by the relevant statute. In some cases, the court enters judgements based on the mediation agreement.

Whether an agreement reached by the parties through a non-adjudicatory process may be enforceable or not will depend upon the intention of the parties; they can maintain that an agreement reached by them shall not be binding or enforceable or they can maintain that such an agreement will be enforceable only after they have obtained advice of legal experts or other professional advisors. In fact, the Family Mediators Association provides for this latter provision. In the absence of any settlement terms in the memorandum it is usually assumed that an unconditional written agreement signed by or on behalf of the parties would be binding on them and enforceable in law. Under English law of contract there is no reason why such an agreement may not be treated as a binding instrument. Settlement of disputes by oral agreements is risky, but if an agreement is reached even on a *"without prejudice"* basis it would be binding on the parties[4].

Any oral agreement reached by the parties may, of course, be promoted to the status of a Tomlin order, in which case derogation from the order will have direct legal consequences on the party in breach of the order. Where a settlement has been recorded as an arbitration award then the usual process of enforcement of such an award may be applied.

Ideally, all terms of settlement should be reduced into writing and the mediator/conciliator must ensure that the terms have received the consent of the parties and that they are clear to them. The mediator/conciliator should also explain to the parties the consequences, particularly, the legal ones of derogating from their agreed terms.

In theory, it is quite possible to make the agreement binding or non-binding in law. Of course, non-binding agreements may lose their value and the time spent on ADR may be wasted. A mediator/conciliator must also ensure that in settling the terms for a binding agreement, the parties have given their consent not under coercion or oppression but by their free will.

The terms of the agreement must not be drafted in a complex form; it should be ensured that the language of a settlement agreement is clear to the parties

[4] See *Rush & Tomkins v Greater London Council and Another* [1989] 1 AC 1280; see further Brown and Marriott at 378

and that legal jargon has been avoided in drafting the terms of settlement. Where, however, a dispute is highly complex; terms of a settlement may have to be drafted under different headings and sub-headings. It would be advisable to take a short period of time to draft the terms of settlement in order to ensure that no gaps have been left and no complexity has been entered into it.

Some of the institutions engaged in the ADR process have developed their own standard form of terms of settlement[5]. If ADR takes place under the auspices of such an institution, parties may like to see in advance the standard form of the terms of settlement adopted by that institution. When a settlement is recorded as an arbitration award it should be drafted as a consent order. Where, however, a mediation process may initially fail to reach a settlement it would be advisable to ask the parties to reflect on what happened during the mediation because in most cases it is during this period that parties seem to realise the root causes of the differences that exist between them. The purpose of giving such an advice is to see whether they would return to mediation. Where mediation results in a partial settlement the positive aspects of such a settlement should not be disregarded in that at least they have reached an agreement on certain matters; therefore they might also make second attempt to resolve the remaining matters. If they should decide to come back, a fresh negotiator or additional experts joining the team might be useful[6].

11.5 CONCLUSIONS

As stated earlier, enforcement of ADR-based settlements should not present any particular difficulty in that it is always possible to enforce such settlements if reduced into writing, under court proceedings. These will be treated as simple contracts. Where ADR is court-related, then hardly any problem of enforcement may be foreseen. In the case of mandatory ADRs which exist, for example, in Australia and the United States, the question of not enforcing the agreed settlement would not arise. In the United Kingdom, court-related ADR, from a psychological standpoint, seems to carry a greater degree of weight and credibility. The Commercial Courts Practice Direction actually requires consideration and discussion of ADR possibility. From a pragmatic standpoint, there is no reason why parties should not abide by their agreed settlement as otherwise they will be required to refer their dispute to courts and in that event the entire purpose of referring the matter to an ADR process will be defeated.

The issue of enforceability in ADR is to be considered from a special point of view, that is, why parties decide to take advantage of the ADR process. From a psychological standpoint, a party seeks a solution to a problem by not resorting

---

5 For example, CEDR or the British Institute of Experts

6 See further K Mackie, D Miles, W Marsh, *Commercial Dispute Resolution, An ADR Practice Guide*, Butterworths, London 1995 at 133

to any court proceedings, in other words, it is inclined to see that a decision is reached by a non-court procedure.

Therefore, there is no reason to assume that any settlement reached under a non-court procedure may not necessarily be effective. If parties wish to settle their dispute by a non-court procedure and wish to be bound by this procedure there is no reason why such a settlement cannot *per se* be binding. Thus, an analogy with the law of contract that an agreement to negotiate is unenforceable may not be rigidly applied to the ADR system. The decision which confirmed that an agreement to negotiate is unenforceable was rendered by the Court of Appeal in *Courtney and Fairbairn Ltd v Tolaini Brothers (Hotels) Ltd*[7]. In that case the Court of Appeal confirmed that:

> *"the letters which were exchanged between the parties did not contain any agreement on the price, nor did they provide for any method for ascertaining the price. They amounted to no more than an agreement to negotiate fair and reasonable contracts sums."*[8]

It must be pointed out however that the *Courtney* case was concerned with the validity of contracts and the legal status of a commercial agreement to negotiate. The ADR system is different from court-based decisions in that parties come to negotiate and the result of negotiation would lead to an agreement. Negotiation is a process to lead to an agreement and therefore the usual principles of the law of contract, that an agreement to negotiate is unenforceable, should not apply to the ADR system.

The other case which is often cited to affirm the non-enforceability of an agreement to negotiate is *Walford and Others v Miles and Others*[9]. In that case the House of Lords decided, inter alia, that *"an agreement to negotiate in good faith for an unspecified period was not enforceable ..."* but this decision is not really applicable to the ADR system when parties come to negotiate their differences. The meaning of an agreement to negotiate a commercial contract and the meaning of negotiating differences between the parties upon clarification with a view to reaching an agreement are two different issues; consequently analogies with these cases may not be relevant.

---

[7] [1975]1 All ER at 716

[8] op. cit., 717

[9] [1992] 1 All ER at 453

CHAPTER 12

Sports-related ADR

12.1 INTRODUCTION

Judicial decisions on sports-related issues are not unknown in England. For example, in 1963 *Eastham v Newcastle United Football Club Ltd and Others*[1] was primarily concerned with the issue of whether the rules of the Football Association and the regulations of the Football League relating to retention and transfer of players was in restraint of trade. The High Court held, inter alia, that:

> *"The combined retention and transfer system as existing at the date of the writ was unreasonable restraint of trade . . ."*[2]

The court did not make any distinction between the application of the principle of the restraint of trade whether in purely commercial matters and in respect of sports-related issues. The principle of the unreasonable restraint of trade must be applied equally. This kind of protection of the injured party can certainly be offered by a court of law. Wilberforce, J (as he then was) stated, inter alia, that:

> *"The employees are just as much affected and, indeed, aimed at by the employers' agreement as the employers themselves. Their liberty of action in seeking employment is threatened just as much as the liberty of the employers to give them employment, and their liberty to seek employment is considered by the law to be an important public interest. Is the defence of that interest to be left exclusively in the hands of the employers themselves, who have set up the ring against the employees and who have (as here) shown every intention of maintaining it as long as they can; left to the chance that one day there may be a blackleg among the employers who will challenge it? In my judgment to grant a remedy by way of declaration to the persons whose interests are vitally affected would be well within the spirit and intent of the rule as to the declaratory judgments."*[3]

Nagle v Feilden and Others[4] was primarily concerned with two legal issues: sex discrimination and restraint of trade. The stewards of the Jockey Club had

---

[1] [1963] 3 ALL ER 140

[2] op. cit., at 140

[3] op. cit., at 155

[4] [1966] 1 ALL ER 689

a monopoly of control over horse-racing in the UK, and in accordance with the unwritten practice refused a woman applicant, a trainer of racehorses, licence. The Court of Appeal held that:

> *"There was an arguable case that by the common law of England there was a right to work at one's trade or profession without being arbitrarily and unreasonably excluded by anyone having the governance of it, that to exclude a woman from being a trainer of race-horses on the ground of her sex, at the present day, would be capricious and unreasonable, and that, therefore, the alleged practice of the stewards was contrary to public policy . . ."*[5]

Lord Denning, MR, raised an important issue in considering this case:

> *". . . if we were here considering a social club, it would be necessary for the plaintiff to show a contract. If a man applies to join a social club and is blackballed, he has no cause of action: because the members have made no contract with him. They can do as they like. They can admit or refuse him, as they please; but we are not considering a social club. We are considering an association which exercises a virtual monopoly in an important field of human activity. By refusing or withdrawing a licence, the stewards can put a man out of business. This is a great power. If it is abused, can the courts give redress?"*[6]

Whether and in what circumstances courts may intervene in providing individuals remedies is the most pertinent issue in considering the limits to the remit of authority to be exercised by non-judicial or private judicial/arbitral/mediation bodies[7]. Lord Denning answered this question by saying that:

> *"It seems to me that this unwritten rule may well be said to be arbitrary and capricious. It is not as if the training of horses could be regarded as an unsuitable occupation for a woman, like that of a jockey or speedway-rider. It is an occupation in which women can and do engage most successfully. It may not be a "vocation" within the Sex Disqualification (Removal) Act, 1919, but still it is an occupation which women can do as well as men, and there would seem to be no reason why they should be excluded from it. If this practice – this unwritten rule – is invalid as being contrary to public policy, there is ground for thinking that the court has jurisdiction to say so. It can make a declaration of right whenever the interest of the plaintiffs is sufficient to justify it."*[8]

Enderby Town Football Club Ltd v Football Association Ltd[9] was predominantly concerned with the issue of natural justice. Indeed, an individual's right

---

[5] ibid.,

[6] op. cit., at 693

[7] The term *"private"* has been used only to indicate that they are not part of the judiciary or the judicial system.

[8] op. cit., at 195; see also *Boulting v Association of Cinematograph, Television and Allied Technicians* [1963] 1 ALL ER 716 at 725, 733

[9] [1971] 1 Ch. 591

to seek remedies against the breach of the rule of natural justice from a court of law can never be denied. Rule 38(b) of the Football Association, which provision was in issue, provided that:

> "... *An association, competition or club may be represented at the hearing of an appeal, complaint or claim or at an enquiry, by one or more of its members. A barrister or solicitor may only represent an association, competition or club of which he is a member, if he be the chairman or secretary. Any person summoned to attend an enquiry or the hearing of an appeal, complaint or claim must attend personally and not be legally represented.*"

The Court of Appeal held that:

> "... *the FA rule 38(b) was not invalid as being contrary to natural justice.*"

However, in this case, Lord Denning, MR, made two interesting comments:

> "*Is a party who is charged before a domestic tribunal entitled as of right to be legally represented? Much depends on what the rules say about it. When the rules say nothing, then the party has no absolute right to be legally represented. It is a matter for the discretion of the tribunal. They are masters of their own procedure; and, if they, in the proper exercise of their discretion, decline to allow legal representation, the courts will not interfere.*"[10]

In support of the services rendered by specialist tribunals composed of specialists, Lord Denning went on to say that:

> "*In many cases it may be a good thing for the proceedings of a domestic tribunal to be conducted informally without legal representation. Justice can often be done in them better by a good lawyer than a bad lawyer. This is especially so in activities like football and other sports, where no points of law are likely to arise, and it is all part of the proper regulation of the game.*"[11]

But, where points of law many arise, the situation may be different. Indeed, Lord Denning warned that:

> "*The tribunal must not fetter its discretion by rigid bonds. A domestic tribunal is not at liberty to lay down an absolute rule.*
>
> ...
>
> *The tribunal must be ready, in a proper case, to allow it. That applies to anyone in authority who is entrusted with a discretion. He must not fetter his discretion by making an absolute rule from which he will never depart.*"[12]

---

[10] op. cit., at 605

[11] op. cit., at 605

[12] ibid.,

Lord Denning further stated that:

> *"It is lawful for a body to stipulate in its rules that its domestic tribunal shall not permit legal representation? Such a stipulation is, I think, clearly valid so long as it is construed as directory and not imperative: for that leaves it open to the tribunal to permit legal representation in an exceptional case when the justice of the case so requires. But I have some doubt whether it is legitimate to make a rule which is so imperative in its terms as to exclude legal representation altogether, without giving the tribunal any discretion to admit it, even when the justice of the case requires it."*[13]

McInnes v Onslow-Fane and Another[14] dealt with an important legal issue regarding an applicant manager's right to be heard in connection with his application for a licence submitted to the British Boxing Board of Control. The plaintiff made six applications for a boxing manager's licence between July 1972 and May 1976, but all had been refused. The plaintiff had previously held a promoter's licence and a master of ceremonies' licence, but in May 1973 all licences had been withdrawn. The plaintiff sought a declaration that in refusing his latest application the Board had acted in breach of natural justice by denying him an oral hearing despite a request made by him to inform him of the case against him so that he could answer it before the Board considered his application.

Megarry, V-C rendered an interesting judgment:

> *"That while there was no contract between the parties and while the case was not one governed by any statute, the case was nevertheless one in which the court was entitled to intervene to enforce the appropriate requirements of natural justice and fairness."*[15]

The court relied on *Nagle v Feilden* and *Enderby Town Football Club Ltd v Football Association Ltd*. In rendering judgment in *McInnes*, the Court raised an issue of a fundamental nature: whether the grant or refusal of a licence by the board was subject of any requirements of natural justice or fairness which would be enforced by the courts. The question was not one that was governed by statute or contracts, with questions of their true construction or the implication of terms, because there was no statute, or any contract between the plaintiff and the Board.

Megarry, V-C further delved into the issue of the right to a fair hearing for the applicant, and his concern for denying that right was clearly evident in the following paragraph:

> *"It seems plain that there is a substantial distinction between the forfeiture cases and the application cases. In the forfeiture cases, there is a threat to take something away for some reason: and in such cases, the right to an unbiased*

[13] op. cit., 607

[14] [1978] 1 WLR 1520

[15] op. cit.,

tribunal, the right to notice of the charges and the right to be heard in answer to the charges (which in Ridge v Baldwin *[1964] A.C. 40, 132, Lord Hodson said were three features of natural justice which stood out) are plainly apt. In the application cases, on the other hand, nothing is being taken away, and in all normal circumstances there are no charges, and so no requirement of an opportunity of being heard in answer to the charges. Instead, there is the far wider and less defined question of the general suitability of the applicant for membership or licence. The distinction is well-recognised, for in general it is clear that the courts will require natural justice to be observed for expulsion from a social club, but not on an application for admission to it. The intermediate category, that of the expectation cases, may at least in some respects be regarded as being more akin to the forfeiture but merely an attempt at acquisition that fails, the legitimate expectation of a renewal of the licence or confirmation of the membership is one which raises the question of what it is that has happened to make the applicant unsuitable for the membership or licence for which he was previously thought suitable."*[16]

Although Megarry, V-C also stated that:

"The Board are the best judges of the desirability of granting the licence, and in the absence of any impropriety the court ought not to interfere."[17]

But his concern about the denial of natural justice was real. The distinction between forfeiture cases and application cases is an important one. In the former type of cases, the right of an applicant to be heard becomes important. The court did not question the integrity or authority of the Board to judge the merits of application; but the denial of the right to be heard is a matter which is concerned with the right of an individual, and this right can only be vindicated by the intervention of a court of law and not by a tribunal. This issue remains important in considering whether ADR authorities should not have limits to their powers, but this is not to suggest that ADR institutions' capacity and the quality of service they render should be questioned. The issue is that one should maintain a distinction between a judicial and non-judicial body.

12.2 SOME OF THE INSTITUTIONS ENGAGED IN RESOLVING SPORTS DISPUTES

It is not possible to discuss all the institutions engaged in resolving sports-related disputes. It has therefore been decided to discuss the most important institutions engaged in resolving such disputes, namely, the Court of Arbitration for Sport (CAS)[18], the International Council of Arbitration for Sport (ICAS), and the UK institution known as the UK Sports Dispute Resolution

[16] op. cit., at 1529

[17] op. cit., at 1535

[18] CAS is also known as TAS (*Tribunal Arbitral du Sport*)

Panel (SDRP)[19]. The contribution of these two institutions to settling sports-related disputes is now discussed.

12.2.1 The Court of Arbitration for Sport (CAS)

The CAS, which is based in Lausanne, Switzerland, was created by the International Olympic Committee (IOC) in 1983, with offices in Sydney (Australia) and New York (USA). The CAS operates as an independent institution in order to offer its users services in the form of settling disputes related to sports. It maintains a list of arbitrators who are chosen for their specialist knowledge of arbitration and sports law.

Every arbitrator shall remain independent of the parties and should any circumstance become likely to affect independence with respect to any of the parties, he must notify the CAS court office immediately. On the grounds of legitimate doubts over his independence, an arbitrator may be challenged, and the ICAS or its board shall rule on the challenge with reason, after considering the comments submitted to it by the challenged arbitrator, the parties, and other invited arbitrators.

An arbitrator may be removed by the ICAS if he refuses to or is prevented from carrying out his duties or fails to fulfil his duties. In the event of an arbitrator being removed, a new arbitrator will be appointed in accordance with the usual provisions applicable to his appointment.

In submitting a reference to arbitration, the party concerned (the proposed Claimant/Applicant) shall file a request with the CAS containing the following information:

(a) the name and address of the Respondent;

(b) a brief statement of the facts and legal arguments therefore, and the issue for the CAS to determine;

(c) the nature of relief that claimant seeks;

(d) a copy of the contact or any other document providing for arbitration; and

(e) the number of arbitrators to be appointed, and if there is a provision for three arbitrators, the name and address of the arbitrator chosen by the Claimant from the CAS list.

If it should appear that there is manifestly no agreement to arbitrate under the auspices of the CAS, the Court Office shall take all appropriate action to set the arbitration in motion. Often communicating the request to the Respondents, the CAS calls upon the parties to indicate clearly the law

[19] Most of the other sports organisations, namely, FIFA, the world governing body of football, the IAAP, the world governing body of athletics have their own arbitral tribunals to settle their respective disputes. It is worth pointing out whether other institutions in respect of particular sports have their own dispute settlement procedures, be they concerned with motor racing or boxing or any other kind of sport or game.

applicable to the merits of the dispute and sets time-limits for the Respondent to file an answer to the request for arbitration, and to provide information on the choice and number of arbitrators, a brief statement of defence, including defence of the lack of jurisdiction, and any counterclaim. If the arbitration agreement does not specify the number of arbitrators, the President of the Division determines the number taking into account the complexity of the dispute and the amount of the claim.

The parties have the prerogative to agree on the method of appointing arbitrators; however, in the absence of such an agreement, arbitrators shall be appointed in accordance with the CAS procedure[20].

In the case of multiparty arbitrations, the CAS forms the Panel in accordance with the method of appointment agreed by all parties and, in the absence of such an agreement, the President of the Division decides on the number of arbitrators in accordance with Rule 40.

Where a third party's participation is intended by a Respondent, it shall so state in its answer, together with the reasons therefor. A time-limit is set by the Court Office for the third party to state its position on the participation, and to submit a response pursuant to Rule 39[21]. A third party may participate in the arbitration if the arbitration agreement requires him to do so or if the other parties agree to his participation in writing.

Opportunities to conciliate their dispute at any time remain open to the parties and any conciliated settlement may be embodied in an arbitral award rendered by the consent of the parties. The principle of confidentiality is strictly observed under the Procedural Rules, and the arbitrators and the CAS undertake not to disclose any information to any third party relating to the dispute or the proceedings. Without the consent of the parties, no award is made public.

Procedure before the Panel

Procedure before the Panel entails a number of stages: written submissions; hearing; evidentiary proceedings ordered by the Panel; expedited procedure; and defence. The set stages are now briefly discussed.

Where appropriate, the President of the Panel, upon receipt of the file, issues directions in connection with the written submissions. Usually, responses are kept to a minimum (one) but if the circumstances so require, one reply and one second response would be accepted. Additional claims may be raised in the response and in the answer to the request, but not thereafter without the consent of the other party. At the stage of submission, the parties are required to submit all written evidence on which they wish to rely; any late submission of written evidence by any party may be allowed only with the consent of the other party, or of the Panel, as exceptional circumstances so permit. The written submissions shall also specify whether the parties would like to call any witnesses and experts.

---

[20] This Procedure may be found in Rule 40.2 of the Rules.

[21] Rule 39 is concerned with the Initiation of Arbitration by the CAS and Answer.

After the exchange of pleadings is closed, the President of the Panel issues directions for the hearing. Like many other tribunals, the Panel also hears the Parties, the witnesses and experts.

Oral submissions must be concise and limited to the pleadings; but the hearings are not public. Minutes of the hearings are maintained. Witnesses, experts and interpreters make statements, answer questions or translate, as the case may be, under oath or affirmation. After consulting the parties, if the Panel considers itself to be sufficiently informed of the subject matter of the disputes, it may not order any hearing.

At the sustainable request of evidence from a party, the Panel may at any time order the production of additional documents; appointment and hearing of experts, if of course, it deems it so appropriate. Experts shall be and remain independent.

With the consent of the parties, the Panel may adopt an expeditious procedure, but it must issue appropriate directions to that effect. If the Claimant should fail to submit its statement of claim in compliance with the procedure, the request for arbitration shall be deemed withdrawn[22]. But, if the Respondent fails to submit its response in advance with the Procedure, *"the Panel may nevertheless proceed with the arbitration and deliver an award."*[23] If neither of the parties fails to appear at the hearing, after being properly summoned, the Panel may still proceed with the hearing.

The Governing Law and the Award

The parties have the freedom to choose the governing law of their dispute; but in the absence of such a choice, the Panel shall decide the dispute according to Swiss law. It is interesting to note that the Code allows the Panel to decide a dispute *ex aequo et bono*, which is a very useful option in that many sports-related disputes may fall squarely within the remit of legislation.

Awards are made by a majority decision, but in the absence of a majority, by the vote of the President alone. All awards must be in writing, dated and signed, and based on reason, unless the parties agree otherwise. Unlike other tribunals, under the Code, the signature of the President of the Panel on the award shall suffice.

An award shall be final and binding upon the parties, and it may not be challenged by way of an action for setting aside.

Appeal

Rule 47 provides that:

> *"A party may appeal from the decision of a disciplinary tribunal or similar body of a federation, association or sports body, insofar as the statutes or regulations of the said body so provide or as the parties have concluded a specific arbitration agreement and insofar as the appellant has exhausted the legal*

---

[22] Rule 44.5

[23] ibid.,

remedies available to him prior to the appeal, in accordance with the statutes or regulations of the said sports body."

A statement of appeal must contain the following: the name and address of the respondent; a copy of the decision appealed against; the nature of relief requested by the appellant; the name of the arbitrator chosen by the appellant from the CAS list; an application to stay the execution of the decision appealed against, if applicable, together with reasons; and a copy of the provisions of the statutes or regulations or agreement allowing appeal to the CAS[24].

Unless any time-limit is set by a relevant statute or the regulations of a federation, association or sports body, an appeal must be lodged within 21 days from the date on which the decision which is appealed against was communicated.

An appeal must be submitted to a Panel of three arbitrators, unless the appellant, at the time of the statement of appeal establishes that the parties agreed to have a Panel composed of a sole arbitrator.

An appeal is deemed withdrawn if an appellant fails to file with the CAS a brief, within ten days following the expiration of the time-limit for the appeal, stating that facts and legal arguments giving rise to the appeal, together with exhibits and evidence on which he intends to rely.

If there is no agreement to arbitrate, the CAS takes appropriate action to set the arbitration in motion, and in that event, the Court communicates the statement of appeal to the respondent, and the President proceeds with the formation of the Panel. The respondent is required to appoint an arbitrator within ten days after the receipt of the statement of appeal.

In the absence of any such appointment the President of the Division proceeds with the appointment. If an appeal is deemed to be one which needs to be considered urgently, it is submitted to a sole arbitrator.

The sole arbitrator is appointed by the President of the Division; he also appoints the President of the Panel. After the Panel is formed, the Court Office transfers the file to the arbitrators.

The respondent is required to take action within twenty days from the date of the receipt of the grounds of appeal in the form of submitting a statement of defence; exhibits and evidence on which it wishes to rely on, and challenge, if any, of the jurisdiction. Parties are not usually allowed to supplement their arguments or produce any more evidence after the stipulated date to do so, unless the parties agree otherwise or the President of the Panel so orders on the grounds of exceptional circumstances. A respondent's failure to do this by the stipulated dated does not prohibit a Panel from proceeding with an arbitration and deliver an award.

The Panel

The Panel shall have full power to review the facts and the law. The President of the Panel shall issue directions in connection with the hearing and

[24] Rule 48.1

examination of the parties, their witnesses and experts. After consulting the parties, it is for the Panel to decide whether or not to hold an oral hearing. However, proceedings take place in camera, unless the parties agree otherwise.

The Panel decides a dispute by applying the law chosen by the parties, but in the absence of any such choice, according to the law of the country in which the federation, association or sports body, which originally rendered the decision, is domiciled.

Awards are rendered by a majority decision, or in the absence of a majority, by the President of the Panel alone. All awards must be written, dated and signed, and based on reasons. The award shall be final and binding upon the parties, and a plan of setting aside of awards on certain grounds are not usually granted[25].

Opinions

Request for an opinion from the CAS on any legal issue in regard to the promotion or development of sports or any activity related to sports may be made by the IOC, the International Sports Federation (ISF), the National Olympic Committees (NOCs), the associations recognised by the IOC, and the Organizing Committee for the Games (OCOG). A request or an opinion is initially reviewed by the President in order to determine whether it may be the subject of an opinion, and if the review is in the affirmative, a Panel of one or three arbitrators from the CAS list is formed, and formulates the questions for consideration by the Panel. An opinion rendered by a Panel is not to be treated as a binding arbitral award.

Parties wishing to refer their dispute to the CAS are required to do so by means of a written agreement. Parties may agree in advance to submit their dispute to CAS or they can conclude an agreement to that effect after a dispute has actually arisen.

Any dispute directly or indirectly linked to sport, commercial or otherwise, or a dispute arising from a decision of a sports organisation may be referred to the CAS. Any natural or artificial person with legal capacity may refer a dispute to the Court of Arbitration for Sport, including, for example, clubs, sponsors, radio or television companies, athletes or sports association.

CAS arbitration procedures entail three forms: (a) the ordinary procedure for disputes arising from contractual relations or wrongful acts; (b) the appeals procedure applicable to disputes emanating from decisions taken by organs of sports federations or associations; and (c) the advisory procedure which is applied when an advisory opinion may be sought by certain bodies or any legal issue concerned with the practice or development of sport or any sport-related activity. Opinions given under the latter procedure do not constitute awards and are not binding.

Ordinary Arbitration

English and French are the languages in which arbitration procedures are conducted, but under certain circumstances another language may be used. A

[25] Rule 59

party need not be represented by a lawyer, although the parties may be represented or assisted at CAS hearings by a person of their choice.

Whereas under the ordinary procedure arbitration is set in motion by sending the CAS Court Office a request for arbitration, a notice of appeal is required to be sent to the same office for activating an appeals procedures. The contents of the request for arbitration and the notice of appeal are specified by the Code of Sports-related Arbitration. A party may lodge an appeal only if it has exhausted all local remedies of the association or federation concerned.

Usually, an arbitration under the CAS procedure is submitted to a panel of three arbitrators; each party chooses an arbitrator from the CAS list, and the third is selected by the two designated arbitrators; the third arbitrator is the President of the Panel. Provided the parties agree or if the CAS deems it more appropriate in the light of the nature of the dispute, a single arbitrator may be appointed. Arbitrators must be independent so that their neutrality may not be questioned. Like many other arbitral procedures, the CAS procedure also requires submission of defence by the Respondent(s)[26], pays attention to exchange of statements of a case, hears the parties, considers evidence produced by both parties, and renders an award.

The parties are free to agree on the law applicable to the merits of the dispute; however, if the parties have failed to agree on the applicable (governing) law, in the case of an ordinary arbitration, Swiss law will apply. Where an appeals procedure is to be followed, *"the arbitrators rule on the basis of the regulations of the federations or associations concerned by the appeal and, subsidarily the law of the country in which the sports body is domiciled."*[27] The Code of Sports-related Arbitration governs the procedure. Whereas the appeals procedure is free, except for an initial fee of Swiss Francs 500, the ordinary procedure entails costs and fees of the arbitrators, in addition to a share of the costs of the CAS.

A case under the ordinary procedure may be settled between 6 and 10 months, but an award under the appeals procedure can, in principle, be pronounced within four months of filing the notice of appeal; however, in urgent cases, the CAS may order interim measures within a very short period of time. The ordinary arbitration procedure is confidential, but the obligation of confidentiality is not specifically stated in respect of the appeals procedure, but the arbitrators and the CAS staff have a duty of confidentiality.

A CAS award is final and binding on the parties, and it may be executed in accordance with the New York Convention on the Recognition and Execution of Arbitral Awards.

---

[26] The CAS procedure describes the Respondents as Defendants.

[27] See http://www.tas-cas.org

12.3 THE MEDIATION RULES OF THE INTERNATIONAL COUNCIL OF ARBITRATION FOR SPORT (ICAS)

12.3.1 General

Mediations conducted under the auspices of the International Council of Arbitration for Sport are known as CAS mediations. The procedure for these mediations is informal; and mediations by CAS are non-binding in nature. A mediation by CAS is based on a mediation agreement in which each party undertakes to negotiate in good faith, with a view to settling their disputes with the assistance of a CAS mediator. This mediation service is available solely for the resolution of disputes coming under the CAS ordinary procedure.

It is believed that a *"dispute"* in this context will stand for any difference between the parties on a sports-related issue which they failed to settle. It is to be emphasised that a decision passed by an organ of a sports organisation cannot be the subject of mediation proceedings before the CAS. Furthermore, disputes arising from disciplinary matters as well as drugs-related issues are beyond the remit of CAS mediation proceedings.

Article 2 of the Mediation Rules defines a mediation agreement as:

> *"A mediation agreement is one whereby the parties agree to submit to mediation a sports-related dispute which has arisen or which may arise between them, A mediation agreement may take the form of a mediation clause inserted in a contract or that of a separate agreement."*

"Submission to mediation" must be understood to the sense of *"submission to arbitration"*; without satisfying the conditions to submitting to mediation, a mediation cannot be activated. Where a mediation agreement provides for mediation under the CAS Mediation Rules, these shall be deemed to form an integral part of the mediation agreement. The parties may however agree to apply other rules of procedure. An applicant is required to address a request, in writing, to the CAS Court Office, sending a copy to the other party, and the request shall contain the identity of the parties, the names and addresses of their representatives, a copy of the mediation agreement, and a brief description of the dispute. The commencement of mediation proceedings is determined by reference to the date on which the request for mediation is received by the CAS.

12.3.2 Appointment of the Mediator

The ICAS develops its list of mediators from the list of CAS arbitrators or from outside. Unless the parties otherwise agree, a mediator shall be chosen by the CAS President from among the list of CAS mediators, and they will be appointed in consultation with the parties. In accepting his appointment, a mediator is required to devote sufficient time to the mediation proceedings. He shall be and must remain independent of the parties. If a mediator should cease his mandate, which is allowed by the parties concerned, because of an objection by any of the parties or at his own discretion if he deems himself unable to bring the mediation to a successful conclusion, he is required to inform the CAS President accordingly, and the latter shall appoint a replacement in consultation with the parties.

12.3.3 Conduct of Mediation and the Role of the Mediator

It is for the parties to agree on the manner in which a mediation should be conducted. In the event of the parties failing to reach an agreement on this matter, the mediator shall determine the manner in which the mediation will be conducted. Representation of parties is allowed, but if a party is represented, the other party and the CAS must be informed of the identity of the representative beforehand. The representative must have full authority to settle the dispute alone, and consultation with the party he represents is not necessary.

As part of his duties, the mediator establishes the terms and timetable for submission by each party, and a statement identifying the facts and points of law in the dispute and a copy of the mediation agreement. Article 8 of the Mediation Rules provides, inter alia, that:

> *"Each party shall cooperate in good faith with the mediator and shall guarantee him the freedom to perform his mandate to advance the mediation as expeditiously as possible."*

A mediator has the right to meet the parties separately, and he may make any suggestions which he may deem appropriate for the purpose of resolving the dispute; but he may not impose a solution to the dispute deemed appropriate by him on any of the parties[28].

Confidentiality is strictly observed in respect of CAS mediation. No record or minutes of any kind are made at meetings. None of the participants – the parties, their representatives, advisers, experts and any other person who may be present during the meetings may not disclose to any third party any information provided to them, unless required by the law to do so. The parties undertake not to compel their mediator to divulge records, reports or other comments to testify in relation to the mediation in any arbitral or judicial proceedings. Any information provided to the mediator by one party may be disclosed by the mediator to the other party only with the consent of the party providing the information. All written documents submitted by the parties must be returned to them without retaining any photocopy or copy of any form thereof. Article 10 of the Mediation Rules provides that:

> *"The parties shall not rely on, or introduce as evidence in any arbitral or judicial proceedings:*
>
> *a. views expressed or suggestions made by a party with respect to a possible settlement of the dispute;*

[28] Article 9 of the Mediation Rules

b. admissions made by a party in the course of the mediation proceedings;

c. documents, notes or other information obtained during the mediation proceedings;

d. proposals made or views expressed by the mediator; or

e. the fact that a party had or has not indicated willingness to accept a proposal."

A mediation may be terminated at any time either by a party or by the mediator. In order for a mediation to terminate, the following procedure must be followed: (a) by signing of a settlement by the parties themselves; or (b) by a written declaration by the mediator himself confirming that further efforts at mediation would not be worthwhile; or (c) by a declaration of a party or both parties to the effect that the mediation proceedings are terminated[29].

The settlement which is to be drawn up by the mediator must be signed by the mediator and the parties. In the event of a breach, a party may rely on the settlement before an arbitral or judicial authority. The CAS Court Office retains a copy of the settlement.

If mediation should fail, the parties may refer their dispute to arbitration, provided that an arbitration agreement or a clause to arbitrate exists. If an arbitration clause is included in the mediation agreement, the expedited procedure under Article 44(4) of the Code of Sport-related Arbitration may be applied[30].

All costs arising from the mediation process will be borne by the parties in equal share.

The Mediation Rules recommend the following clause for CAS mediation, which may be incorporated in a contract:

"Any dispute, any controversy or claim arising under, out of or relating to this contract and any subsequent amendments of or in relation to this contract, including, but not limited to, its formation, validity, binding effect, interpretation, performance, breach or termination, as well as non-contractual claims, shall be submitted to mediation in accordance with the CAS Mediation Rules. The language to be used in the mediation shall be ..."

Additional clause in the absence of settlement of the dispute:

"If, and to the extent that, any such dispute has not been settled within 90 days of the commencement of the mediation, or if, before the expiration of the said period, either party fails to participate or continue to participate in the mediation, the dispute shall, upon the filing of a Request for Arbitration by either party, be referred to and finally settled by CAS arbitration pursuant to the Code of Sports-related Arbitration. When the circumstances so require, the mediator

[29] Article 11

[30] Article 44(4)

> *may, at his own discretion or at the request of a party, seek an extension of the time limit from the CAS President."*

The CAS mediation procedure and rules are very similar to those of similar institutions offering mediation services. The confidentiality provisions in the CAS mediation seem to be comprehensive. However, the recommended clause for CAS mediation seems to be extremely broad; furthermore, the use of certain terms, namely any dispute arising *"out of"* or *"relating to"* or *"in relation to this contract"*, might provoke controversy. Disparities or controversy usually arise under or out of a contract, rather than *"relating to"* or *"in relation"* to a contract[31].

12.4 COSTS

12.4.1 Ordinary Arbitration

Requests for ordinary arbitrations are to be made with a minimum non-refundable fee of Swiss Francs 500 to the CAS Court Office. The Panels takes this amount into account when assessing the final amount of the fees. Upon formation of the Panel, the Court Office determines the amount and the method of payment of the advance of costs. In determining this amount of advance, the Court Office estimates the costs of arbitration, which are to be borne by the parties, and the advance must be paid in equal shares by the Claimant and the Respondent. If a party should fail to pay its share, the other party may substitute for it and, in the absence of substitution, the claim to which the unpaid share relates is deemed withdrawn[32]. The costs of requiring its witnesses, experts and interpreters shall be borne by each party. In the event of the Panel wishing to appoint an expert or retaining an interpreter or ordering the examination of a witness, it issues directions in regard to advance of costs, if appropriate.

At the end of the proceedings, the Court Office determines the final amount of the costs of arbitration, which includes the CAS Court Office fee, the costs and fees of the arbitrators, the contribution towards the costs and expenses of the CAS, in addition to the costs of witnesses, experts and interpreters. The costs are shown in arbitral awards indicating which party shall bear what amount of costs. In general, the Rules state that:

> *"... the award shall grant the prevailing party a contribution towards its legal fees and other expenses incurred in connection with the proceedings and, in particular, the costs of witnesses and interpreters. When granting such contribution, the Panel shall take into account the outcome of the proceedings as well as the conduct and the financial resources of the parties."*[33]

[31] See further, S K Chatterjee, "Do Disputes arise 'out of' or 'under' or 'out of and under' a Contract?", *Arbitration*, May 1994 at 117–122

[32] Rule 64.2

[33] Rule 64.5

12.4.2 Appeal Arbitration

Unless otherwise required, the proceedings are free. Where costs are entailed, the fees and costs of the arbitrators are calculated in accordance with the CAS fee scale together with the costs of the CAS are borne by the CAS. Upon submission of the statement of appeal, the appellant is required to pay to the Court Office a minimum fee of Swiss Francs 500; this fee is non-refundable. The costs of the parties, witnesses, experts and interpreters are advanced by the parties. The Panel states in the award which party would be required to bear what amount of costs, and in what proportion, taking into account the outcome of the proceedings, as well as the conduct and financial resources of the parties[34].

12.4.3 Consultation Proceedings

The costs of consultation proceedings are determined by the CAS Court Office after consultation with the party requesting an opinion.

12.5 CONCLUSIONS

The Court of Arbitration for Sports (CAS) was set up with a view to settle sports-related disputes with the help of experts in the field of sports. It has two Divisions: the Ordinary Arbitration Division and the Appeals Division: disputes are allocated to one of these depending on their nature. Basically, under the ordinary arbitration method come disputes which are fit for the ordinary arbitration procedure; whereas disputes which come in the form of appeals are referred to the appeals arbitration method.

The CAS offers a unique service in regard to sports-related disputes in that parties from any jurisdiction may refer their disputes to it and they can choose the governing law of their dispute, however, in the absence of the parties' choice, Swiss law will be the governing law. Furthermore, the CAS applies the procedure based on a Code of Sports-related Arbitration; this means that the parties are not governed by the procedural law of Lausanne, where the CAS is located. This makes arbitrations more acceptable than those which are governed by the law of the forum of arbitration.

CAS arbitrators are chosen from a list of people who are known for their competence in legal matters and who possess *"sound knowledge of the problems concerned with sports activity."*[35]

As disputes are settled by people who have knowledge in sports-related activity, the awards rendered by them are expected to be more enforced than judgments rendered by courts. The procedures for both ordinary arbitration (which is initiated by an application stating reasons), and appeals arbitration (which may be initiated by a simple statement of appeal, justified by reasons)

[34] Rule 65.3

[35] *Guide to Arbitration* published by CAS, Lausanne (undated) at 7.

are simple, and the parties may choose their arbitrators from a list published by the ICAS (the International Council of Arbitration for Sport). Although the working languages of the CAS are English and French, parties to a dispute may agree to use another language for the proceedings; this is satisfactory for parties, and also not so time-consuming as it does not require the services of any interpreters. The parties may appear themselves before the CAS or be represented by a person of their choice.

Bearing in mind that an athlete's career is relatively short, the CAS makes every effort to settle disputes as quickly as possible. In urgent cases, its procedure allows it to grant interim measures. The CAS is the court of first instance and the court of final instance; its awards are final and enforceable, and very limited possibilities of appeal are provided to parties.

It has already been explained that the CAS places utmost importance upon the issue of confidentiality. Compared to other arbitral tribunals, the CAS charges minimally for settling disputes. It is to be re-iterated that in respect of appeals procedure, the fees and expenses of arbitrators and the CAS costs are usually by the CAS.

As examples of issues that are usually referred to its ordinary arbitration procedure, mention may be made of sponsorship contracts; contracts between athletes and managers; contracts for granting of television rights to a sports event; issues of third party liability.

Examples of issues/disputes which are usually submitted to the appeals procedure are: decision taken by other sports tribunals, associations or other sports-bodies; and issues and matters which are allowed to be appealed against by the statutes and regulations of specific associations or sports-bodies.

The CAS services may be availed of by any individual or legal entity having full legal capacity.

In order for a dispute to be referred to the CAS, parties must agree to do so, and this agreement may take one of the following forms:

(a) if a CAS arbitration clause has been included in a contract; or the clause has been agreed upon by the parties (usually in the form of a *compromis*) after a dispute has already arisen;

(b) for disputes relating to decisions made by sports bodies, the sports body or federation concerned, an arbitration clause in its statutes or regulations has been incorporated, and the athlete has adhered to this clause, in writing. The CAS recommends that the adherence makes specific reference to arbitration by CAS.

In the absence of any specific prior agreement, the CAS may also assume jurisdiction on the basis of an agreement concluded or an ad hoc basis by the parties concerned.

In order to ensure prompt resolution of dispute CAS maintain a rather rigid policy as to the extension of time-limits, particularly those fixed by the Procedural Rules. The time-limits fixed by the CAS Court Office, the

President of the Panel and the President of the Division concerned may be extended provided an application for an extension of the time-limit is supported by sustainable reasons[36].

The nature of proceedings, both ordinary and appeal has been explained; however it is worth pointing out that the CAS proceedings time is of essence. The procedures which are maintained by the CAS are not significantly different from those followed by similar tribunals. Like many other arbitral tribunals, (namely, those organised under the auspices of the International Chamber of Commerce or under the English Arbitration Act 1996) CAS arbitral tribunal have the power to grant interim measures of protection. One of the important aspects of the CAS awards is that if one of the parties refuses to execute the award voluntarily, the other party may obtain its execution by initiating exequatur proceedings before national courts of the place of execution. In many cases, the New York Convention on the Recognition and Enforcement of Foreign Arbitral Awards, 1958 will govern the enforcement of awards in most cases, as many states are parties to this Convention. A CAS award is final and binding and may not be challenged or appealed against unless in very exceptional circumstances an annulment appeal is lodged (examples of such exceptional circumstances would be: incompetence of the arbitration Panel; or irregular constitution of the Panel; or the award is contrary to the mandatory principles and policies of the jurisdiction concerned). Incidentally, the time-limit for challenging an award is thirty days from the date on which the award was communicated, and the Swiss Federal Tribunal acts as the Court of Appeal.

The system of rendering advisory opinion is laudable in that such opinion may clarify the position of parties, and may lessen the incidence of arbitration.

[36] See further Rule 32

CONCLUSIONS

Informal dispute resolution practices have been with the international community for a long time; in fact, dispute settlements at market places by the so-called arbitration system may be regarded as an alternative dispute resolution method.

Since 1990, ADR as a method of settling disputes outside the court system has attained popularity, particularly because of the perception that disputes of any nature may be settled in a friendly environment without the formalities through which court proceedings usually advance. This work maintains that whereas ADR may be very effective in respect of certain types of dispute, namely, matrimonial or family-related disputes, ADR can be as formal as court proceedings in setting commercial disputes of a commercial nature.

It is important to bear in mind that ADR system is also based on procedure; it can be formal; and parties to a dispute may develop the kind of apprehension that they often develop in respect of court proceedings. Whenever a dispute involves resolution of legal issues, dispute resolution is required to follow a procedure and the discussion will become formal. Hence the controversy arises whether ADR is fundamentally different from court proceedings. This controversy will persist for some time to come. The psychological satisfaction of parties from an informal system of settling disputes or differences is at the root of this controversy. Societies are still used to the coercive system of adjudication of disputes by courts of law in a formal atmosphere, which, in their view, provides a sufficient degree of acceptability of judgments. Furthermore, the perception exists that disputes, if not differences, should be settled by an application of the law by judges appointed by the State. The characteristics of the English common law system, in particular are formidable: certainty, predictability and judicial neutrality.

ADR can be successful in relation to family-related or matrimonial matters, as these are essentially fact- or conduct-based disputes, or disputes relating to apportionment of assets or the protection of children. In respect of employment-related disputes, ACAS' intervention, as a form of ADR, sometimes proves effective, particularly when disputes relate to the conduct of the employer or employee, and the procedural defects under the law in dealing with matters through ADR as a preliminary to court proceedings are worth trying. If the parties fail to resolve their dispute at this stage, at least they will have a second opportunity to appreciate the legal issues involved in their disagreement, and decide whether they should proceed with their dispute at all, or negotiate with the other side. Complex legal disputes settled by ADR method, can be less *"time- and money-consuming"*.

Perhaps the success of ADR depends on the attitude of parties towards dispute settlement; that is, how willing they are to settle it by an amicable and less cumbersome method. Public awareness of the effectiveness of ADR should be created; the issue is not whether the judicial system of a country has made ADR a component of justice; the participatory nature of dispute settlement is one of the most important features of ADR.

In the event of the agreed decision of the parties not being enforced, the court procedure for enforcing judgments still remains. Mutually agreed decisions have contractual effect, a breach of which may give rise to a cause of action.

However, certain types of dispute of a complex nature, for example, disputes related to the conduct of a player on a stock exchange or breach of intellectual property rights or admiralty issues may not be entirely suitable for the ADR system.

ADR system is not entirely law-free or procedure-free. Parties are required to be aware of their legal rights and remedies; thus, assistance of or support from legal representatives often proves necessary in going through an ADR system. In England, parties are still required to express their views or points through their legal representatives when a dispute is referred to an ADR system. Although the chairman allocated to a case may not be a formal judge, the parties are advised to follow the procedure set / explained by the chairman. Indeed, like court proceedings, parties or courts referring their disputes to ADR are required to prepare and submit their papers in the same way as for court proceedings. Usually, examination and cross-examination of witnesses are avoided. All members having interest in the subject matter of the dispute or concerned with the dispute may be present at an ADR session, and they must confide with their legal representatives unless, of course, a party has decided to appear in person to present his/her/its case before the chairman. Failure to settle a dispute through an ADR system entails costs and time. Should they wish to proceed with their dispute for a settlement through court proceedings, they must be prepared for further legal costs.

ADR certainly provides a test ground to determine whether or not to proceed with the claim or the defence. Parties will have an opportunity to learn through oral statements each other's arguments and why they may or may not be prepared to settle there and then, and would be prepared to go through court proceedings. Alternatively, after an ADR session, parties may reflect on their respective case, and finally decide to settle, instead of going through court proceedings.

In order to make ADR a successful method of settling disputes the judiciary of a country must accord full recognition to it, as well as drawing public attention to the purposes and effectiveness of this method of dispute resolution.

APPENDIX I

WIPO Mediation Rules*

ABBREVIATED EXPRESSIONS

Article 1

In these Rules:

"Mediation Agreement" means an agreement by the parties to submit to mediation all or certain disputes which have arisen or which may arise between them; a Mediation Agreement may be in the form of a mediation clause in a contract or in the form of a separate contract;
"Mediator" includes a sole mediator or all the mediators where more than one is appointed;
"WIPO" means the World Intellectual Property Organization;
"Center" means the WIPO Arbitration and Mediation Center, a unit of the International Bureau of WIPO;
Words used in the singular include the plural and vice versa, as the context may require.

SCOPE OF APPLICATION OF RULES

Article 2

Where a Mediation Agreement provides for mediation under the WIPO Mediation Rules, these Rules shall be deemed to form part of that Mediation Agreement. Unless the parties have agreed otherwise, these Rules as in effect on the date of the commencement of the mediation shall apply.

COMMENCEMENT OF THE MEDIATION

Article 3

(a) A party to a Mediation Agreement that wishes to commence a mediation shall submit a Request for Mediation in writing to the Center. It shall at the same time send a copy of the Request for Mediation to the other party.

---

* The author gives due thanks and acknowledgement to the World Intellectual Property Organization (WIPO) for permission to reproduce the WIPO Mediation Rules.

(b) The Request for Mediation shall contain or be accompanied by:
(i) the names, addresses and telephone, telefax, e-mail or other communication references of the parties to the dispute and of the representative of the party filing the Request for Mediation;
(ii) a copy of the Mediation Agreement; and
(iii) a brief statement of the nature of the dispute.

Article 4

The date of the commencement of the mediation shall be the date on which the Request for Mediation is received by the Center.

Article 5

The Center shall forthwith inform the parties in writing of the receipt by it of the Request for Mediation and of the date of the commencement of the mediation.

APPOINTMENT OF THE MEDIATOR

Article 6

(a) Unless the parties have agreed themselves on the person of the mediator or on another procedure for appointing the mediator, the mediator shall be appointed by the Center after consultation with the parties.
(b) The prospective mediator shall, by accepting appointment, be deemed to have undertaken to make available sufficient time to enable the mediation to be conducted expeditiously.

Article 7

The mediator shall be neutral, impartial and independent.

REPRESENTATION OF PARTIES AND PARTICIPATION IN MEETINGS

Article 8

(a) The parties may be represented or assisted in their meetings with the mediator.
(b) Immediately after the appointment of the mediator, the names and addresses of persons authorized to represent a party, and the names and positions of the persons who will be attending the meetings of the parties with the mediator on behalf of that party, shall be communicated by that party to the other party, the mediator and the Center.

CONDUCT OF THE MEDIATION

Article 9

The mediation shall be conducted in the manner agreed by the parties. If, and to the extent that, the parties have not made such agreement, the mediator shall, in accordance with these Rules, determine the manner in which the mediation shall be conducted.

Article 10

Each party shall cooperate in good faith with the mediator to advance the mediation as expeditiously as possible.

Article 11

The mediator shall be free to meet and to communicate separately with a party on the clear understanding that information given at such meetings and in such communications shall not be disclosed to the other party without the express authorization of the party giving the information.

Article 12

(a) As soon as possible after being appointed, the mediator shall, in consultation with the parties, establish a timetable for the submission by each party to the mediator and to the other party of a statement summarizing the background of the dispute, the party's interests and contentions in relation to the dispute and the present status of the dispute, together with such other information and materials as the party considers necessary for the purposes of the mediation and, in particular, to enable the issues in dispute to be identified.
(b) The mediator may at any time during the mediation suggest that a party provide such additional information or materials as the mediator deems useful.
(c) Any party may at any time submit to the mediator, for consideration by the mediator only, written information or materials which it considers to be confidential. The mediator shall not, without the written authorization of that party, disclose such information or materials to the other party.

ROLE OF THE MEDIATOR

Article 13

(a) The mediator shall promote the settlement of the issues in dispute between the parties in any manner that the mediator believes to be appropriate, but shall have no authority to impose a settlement on the parties.
(b) Where the mediator believes that any issues in dispute between the parties are not susceptible to resolution through mediation, the mediator may propose, for the consideration of the parties, procedures or means for resolving those issues which the mediator considers are most likely, having regard to the circumstances of the dispute and any business relationship between the

parties, to lead to the most efficient, least costly and most productive settlement of those issues. In particular, the mediator may so propose:

(i) an expert determination of one or more particular issues;

(ii) arbitration;

(iii) the submission of last offers of settlement by each party and, in the absence of a settlement through mediation, arbitration conducted on the basis of those last offers pursuant to an arbitral procedure in which the mission of the arbitral tribunal is confined to determining which of the last offers shall prevail; or

(iv) arbitration in which the mediator will, with the express consent of the parties, act as sole arbitrator, it being understood that the mediator may, in the arbitral proceedings, take into account information received during the mediation.

CONFIDENTIALITY

Article 14

No recording of any kind shall be made of any meetings of the parties with the mediator.

Article 15

Each person involved in the mediation, including, in particular, the mediator, the parties and their representatives and advisors, any independent experts and any other persons present during the meetings of the parties with the mediator, shall respect the confidentiality of the mediation and may not, unless otherwise agreed by the parties and the mediator, use or disclose to any outside party any information concerning, or obtained in the course of, the mediation. Each such person shall sign an appropriate confidentiality undertaking prior to taking part in the mediation.

Article 16

Unless otherwise agreed by the parties, each person involved in the mediation shall, on the termination of the mediation, return, to the party providing it, any brief, document or other materials supplied by a party, without retaining any copy thereof. Any notes taken by a person concerning the meetings of the parties with the mediator shall be destroyed on the termination of the mediation.

Article 17

Unless otherwise agreed by the parties, the mediator and the parties shall not introduce as evidence or in any manner whatsoever in any judicial or arbitration proceeding:

(i) any views expressed or suggestions made by a party with respect to a possible settlement of the dispute;

(ii) any admissions made by a party in the course of the mediation;

(iii) any proposals made or views expressed by the mediator;
(iv) the fact that a party had or had not indicated willingness to accept any proposal for settlement made by the mediator or by the other party.

TERMINATION OF THE MEDIATION

Article 18

The mediation shall be terminated:
(i) by the signing of a settlement agreement by the parties covering any or all of the issues in dispute between the parties;
(ii) by the decision of the mediator if, in the mediator's judgment, further efforts at mediation are unlikely to lead to a resolution of the dispute; or
(iii) by a written declaration of a party at any time after attending the first meeting of the parties with the mediator and before the signing of any settlement agreement.

Article 19

(a) Upon the termination of the mediation, the mediator shall promptly send to the Center a notice in writing that the mediation is terminated and shall indicate the date on which it terminated, whether or not the mediation resulted in a settlement of the dispute and, if so, whether the settlement was full or partial. The mediator shall send to the parties a copy of the notice so addressed to the Center.
(b) The Center shall keep the said notice of the mediator confidential and shall not, without the written authorization of the parties, disclose either the existence or the result of the mediation to any person.
(c) The Center may, however, include information concerning the mediation in any aggregate statistical data that it publishes concerning its activities, provided that such information does not reveal the identity of the parties or enable the particular circumstances of the dispute to be identified.

Article 20

Unless required by a court of law or authorized in writing by the parties, the mediator shall not act in any capacity whatsoever, otherwise than as a mediator, in any pending or future proceedings, whether judicial, arbitral or otherwise, relating to the subject matter of the dispute.

ADMINISTRATION FEE

Article 21

(a) The Request for Mediation shall be subject to the payment to the Center of an administration fee, the amount of which shall be fixed in accordance with the Schedule of Fees applicable on the date of the Request for Mediation.
(b) The administration fee shall not be refundable.

(c) No action shall be taken by the Center on a Request for Mediation until the administration fee has been paid.
(d) If a party who has filed a Request for Mediation fails, within 15 days after a second reminder in writing from the Center, to pay the administration fee, it shall be deemed to have withdrawn its Request for Mediation.

FEES OF THE MEDIATOR

Article 22

(a) The amount and currency of the fees of the mediator and the modalities and timing of their payment shall be fixed by the Center, after consultation with the mediator and the parties.
(b) The amount of the fees shall, unless the parties and the mediator agree otherwise, be calculated on the basis of the hourly or, if applicable, daily indicative rates set out in the Schedule of Fees applicable on the date of the Request for Mediation, taking into account the amount in dispute, the complexity of the subject matter of the dispute and any other relevant circumstances of the case.

DEPOSITS

Article 23

(a) The Center may, at the time of the appointment of the mediator, require each party to deposit an equal amount as an advance for the costs of the mediation, including, in particular, the estimated fees of the mediator and the other expenses of the mediation. The amount of the deposit shall be determined by the Center.
(b) The Center may require the parties to make supplementary deposits.
(c) If a party fails, within 15 days after a second reminder in writing from the Center, to pay the required deposit, the mediation shall be deemed to be terminated. The Center shall, by notice in writing, inform the parties and the mediator accordingly and indicate the date of termination.
(d) After the termination of the mediation, the Center shall render an accounting to the parties of any deposits made and return any unexpended balance to the parties or require the payment of any amount owing from the parties.

COSTS

Article 24

Unless the parties agree otherwise, the administration fee, the fees of the mediator and all other expenses of the mediation, including, in particular, the required travel expenses of the mediator and any expenses associated with obtaining expert advice, shall be borne in equal shares by the parties.

EXCLUSION OF LIABILITY

Article 25

Except in respect of deliberate wrongdoing, the mediator, WIPO and the Center shall not be liable to any party for any act or omission in connection with any mediation conducted under these Rules.

WAIVER OF DEFAMATION

Article 26

The parties and, by accepting appointment, the mediator agree that any statements or comments, whether written or oral, made or used by them or their representatives in preparation for or in the course of the mediation shall not be relied upon to found or maintain any action for defamation, libel, slander or any related complaint, and this Article may be pleaded as a bar to any such action.

SUSPENSION OF RUNNING OF LIMITATION PERIOD UNDER THE STATUTE OF LIMITATIONS

Article 27

The parties agree that, to the extent permitted by the applicable law, the running of the limitation period under the Statute of Limitations or an equivalent law shall be suspended in relation to the dispute that is the subject of the mediation from the date of the commencement of the mediation until the date of the termination of the mediation.

APPENDIX II

ICSID Convention, Regulations and Rules*

CONCILIATION RULES

Chapter I: Establishment of the Commission

Rule 1: General Obligations

(1) Upon notification of the registration of the request for conciliation, the parties shall, with all possible dispatch, proceed to constitute a Commission, with due regard to Section 2 of Chapter III of the Convention.
(2) Unless such information is provided in the request, the parties shall communicate to the Secretary-General as soon as possible any provisions agreed by them regarding the number of conciliators and the method of their appointment.

Rule 2: Method of Constituting the Commission in the Absence of Previous Agreement

(1) If the parties, at the time of the registration of the request for conciliation, have not agreed upon the number of conciliators and the method of their appointment, they shall, unless they agree otherwise, follow the following procedure:

(a) the requesting party shall, within 10 days after the registration of the request, propose to the other party the appointment of a sole conciliator or of a specified uneven number of conciliators and specify the method proposed for their appointment;

(b) within 20 days after receipt of the proposals made by the requesting party, the other party shall:

(i) accept such proposals; or

(ii) make other proposals regarding the number of conciliators and the method of their appointment;

(c) within 20 days after receipt of the reply containing any such other proposals, the requesting party shall notify the other party whether it accepts or rejects such proposals.

(2) The communications provided for in paragraph (1) shall be made or promptly confirmed in writing and shall either be transmitted through the

* The author gives due thanks and acknowledgement to the World Bank for permission to reproduce the ICSID Convention, Regulations and Rules, as they appear on the ICSID website: http://icsid.worldbank.org/ICSID/StaticFiles/basicdoc/partE.htm.

Secretary-General or directly between the parties with a copy to the Secretary-General. The parties shall promptly notify the Secretary-General of the contents of any agreement reached.
(3) At any time 60 days after the registration of the request, if no agreement on another procedure is reached, either party may inform the Secretary-General that it chooses the formula provided for in Article 29(2)(b) of the Convention. The Secretary-General shall thereupon promptly inform the other party that the Commission is to be constituted in accordance with that Article.

Rule 3: Appointment of Conciliators to a Commission Constituted in Accordance with Convention Article 29(2)(b)

(1) If the Commission is to be constituted in accordance with Article 29(2)(b) of the Convention:
(a) either party shall, in a communication to the other party:
(i) name two persons, identifying one of them as the conciliator appointed by it and the other as the conciliator proposed to be the President of the Commission; and
(ii) invite the other party to concur in the appointment of the conciliator proposed to be the President of the Commission and to appoint another conciliator;
(b) promptly upon receipt of this communication the other party shall, in its reply:
(i) name a person as the conciliator appointed by it; and
(ii) concur in the appointment of the conciliator proposed to be the President of the Commission or name another person as the conciliator proposed to be President;
(c) promptly upon receipt of the reply containing such a proposal, the initiating party shall notify the other party whether it concurs in the appointment of the conciliator proposed by that party to be the President of the Commission.
(2) The communications provided for in this Rule shall be made or promptly confirmed in writing and shall either be transmitted through the Secretary-General or directly between the parties with a copy to the Secretary-General.

Rule 4: Appointment of Conciliators by the Chairman of the Administrative Council

(1) If the Commission is not constituted within 90 days after the dispatch by the Secretary-General of the notice of registration, or such other period as the parties may agree, either party may, through the Secretary-General, address to the Chairman of the Administrative Council a request in writing to appoint the conciliator or conciliators not yet appointed and to designate a conciliator to be the President of the Commission.

(2) The provision of paragraph (1) shall apply *mutatis mutandis* in the event that the parties have agreed that the conciliators shall elect the President of the Commission and they fail to do so.
(3) The Secretary-General shall forthwith send a copy of the request to the other party.
(4) The Chairman shall use his best efforts to comply with that request within 30 days after its receipt. Before he proceeds to make an appointment or designation, with due regard to Article 31(1) of the Convention, he shall consult both parties as far as possible.
(5) The Secretary-General shall promptly notify the parties of any appointment or designation made by the Chairman.

Rule 5: Acceptance of Appointments

(1) The party or parties concerned shall notify the Secretary-General of the appointment of each conciliator and indicate the method of his appointment.
(2) As soon as the Secretary-General has been informed by a party or the Chairman of the Administrative Council of the appointment of a conciliator, he shall seek an acceptance from the appointee.
(3) If a conciliator fails to accept his appointment within 15 days, the Secretary-General shall promptly notify the parties, and if appropriate the Chairman, and invite them to proceed to the appointment of another conciliator in accordance with the method followed for the previous appointment.

Rule 6: Constitution of the Commission

(1) The Commission shall be deemed to be constituted and the proceeding to have begun on the date the Secretary-General notifies the parties that all the conciliators have accepted their appointment.
(2) Before or at the first session of the Commission, each conciliator shall sign a declaration in the following form:
"To the best of my knowledge there is no reason why I should not serve on the Conciliation Commission constituted by the International Centre for Settlement of Investment Disputes with respect to a dispute between ________________and ________________.
"I shall keep confidential all information coming to my knowledge as a result of my participation in this proceeding, as well as the contents of any report drawn up by the Commission.
"I shall not accept any instruction or compensation with regard to the proceeding from any source except as provided in the Convention on the Settlement of Investment Disputes between States and Nationals of Other States and in the Regulations and Rules made pursuant thereto.
"A statement of my past and present professional, business and other relationships (if any) with the parties is attached hereto."

Any conciliator failing to sign such a declaration by the end of the first session of the Commission shall be deemed to have resigned.

Rule 7: Replacement of Conciliators

At any time before the Commission is constituted, each party may replace any conciliator appointed by it and the parties may by common consent agree to replace any conciliator. The procedure of such replacement shall be in accordance with Rules 1, 5 and 6.

Rule 8: Incapacity or Resignation of Conciliators

(1) If a conciliator becomes incapacitated or unable to perform the duties of his office, the procedure in respect of the disqualification of conciliators set forth in Rule 9 shall apply.
(2) A conciliator may resign by submitting his resignation to the other members of the Commission and the Secretary-General. If the conciliator was appointed by one of the parties, the Commission shall promptly consider the reasons for his resignation and decide whether it consents thereto. The Commission shall promptly notify the Secretary-General of its decision.

Rule 9: Disqualification of Conciliators

(1) A party proposing the disqualification of a conciliator pursuant to Article 57 of the Convention shall promptly, and in any event before the Commission first recommends terms of settlement of the dispute to the parties or when the proceeding is closed (whichever occurs earlier), file its proposal with the Secretary-General, stating its reasons therefor.
(2) The Secretary-General shall forthwith:
  (a) transmit the proposal to the members of the Commission and, if it relates to a sole conciliator or to a majority of the members of the Commission, to the Chairman of the Administrative Council; and
  (b) notify the other party of the proposal.
(3) The conciliator to whom the proposal relates may, without delay, furnish explanations to the Commission or the Chairman, as the case may be.
(4) Unless the proposal relates to a majority of the members of the Commission, the other members shall promptly consider and vote on the proposal in the absence of the conciliator concerned. If those members are equally divided, they shall, through the Secretary-General, promptly notify the Chairman of the proposal, of any explanation furnished by the conciliator concerned and of their failure to reach a decision.
(5) Whenever the Chairman has to decide on a proposal to disqualify a conciliator, he shall use his best efforts to take that decision within 30 days after he has received the proposal.
(6) The proceeding shall be suspended until a decision has been taken on the proposal.

Rule 10: Procedure during a Vacancy on the Commission

(1) The Secretary-General shall forthwith notify the parties and, if necessary, the Chairman of the Administrative Council of the disqualification, death, incapacity or resignation of a conciliator and of the consent, if any, of the Commission to a resignation.
(2) Upon the notification by the Secretary-General of a vacancy on the Commission, the proceeding shall be or remain suspended until the vacancy has been filled.

Rule 11: Filling Vacancies on the Commission

(1) Except as provided in paragraph (2), a vacancy resulting from the disqualification, death, incapacity or resignation of a conciliator shall be promptly filled by the same method by which his appointment had been made.
(2) In addition to filling vacancies relating to conciliators appointed by him, the Chairman of the Administrative Council shall appoint a person from the Panel of Conciliators:

(a) to fill a vacancy caused by the resignation, without the consent of the Commission, of a conciliator appointed by a party; or
(b) at the request of either party, to fill any other vacancy, if no new appointment is made and accepted within 45 days of the notification of the vacancy by the Secretary-General.

(3) The procedure for filling a vacancy shall be in accordance with Rules 1, 4(4), 4(5), 5 and, *mutatis mutandis*, 6(2).

Rule 12: Resumption of Proceeding after Filling a Vacancy

As soon as a vacancy on the Commission has been filled, the proceeding shall continue from the point it had reached at the time the vacancy occurred. The newly appointed conciliator may, however, require that any hearings be repeated in whole or in part.

CHAPTER II: WORKING OF THE COMMISSION

Rule 13: Sessions of the Commission

(1) The Commission shall hold its first session within 60 days after its constitution or such other period as the parties may agree. The dates of that session shall be fixed by the President of the Commission after consultation with its members and the Secretary-General. If upon its constitution the Commission has no President because the parties have agreed that the President shall be elected by its members, the Secretary-General shall fix the dates of that session. In both cases, the parties shall be consulted as far as possible.
(2) The dates of subsequent sessions shall be determined by the Commission, after consultation with the Secretary-General and with the parties as far as possible.

(3) The Commission shall meet at the seat of the Centre or at such other place as may have been agreed by the parties in accordance with Article 63 of the Convention. If the parties agree that the proceeding shall be held at a place other than the Centre or an institution with which the Centre has made the necessary arrangements, they shall consult with the Secretary-General and request the approval of the Commission. Failing such approval, the Commission shall meet at the seat of the Centre.
(4) The Secretary-General shall notify the members of the Commission and the parties of the dates and place of the sessions of the Commission in good time.

Rule 14: Sittings of the Commission

(1) The President of the Commission shall conduct its hearings and preside at its deliberations.
(2) Except as the parties otherwise agree, the presence of a majority of the members of the Commission shall be required at its sittings.
(3) The President of the Commission shall fix the date and hour of its sittings.

Rule 15: Deliberations of the Commission

(1) The deliberations of the Commission shall take place in private and remain secret.
(2) Only members of the Commission shall take part in its deliberations. No other person shall be admitted unless the Commission decides otherwise.

Rule 16: Decisions of the Commission

(1) Decisions of the Commission shall be taken by a majority of the votes of all its members. Abstention shall count as a negative vote.
(2) Except as otherwise provided by these Rules or decided by the Commission, it may take any decision by correspondence among its members, provided that all of them are consulted. Decisions so taken shall be certified by the President of the Commission.

Rule 17: Incapacity of the President

If at any time the President of the Commission should be unable to act, his functions shall be performed by one of the other members of the Commission, acting in the order in which the Secretary-General had received the notice of their acceptance of their appointment to the Commission.

Rule 18: Representation of the Parties

(1) Each party may be represented or assisted by agents, counsel or advocates whose names and authority shall be notified by that party to the Secretary-General, who shall promptly inform the Commission and the other party.

(2) For the purposes of these Rules, the expression "party" includes, where the context so admits, an agent, counsel or advocate authorized to represent that party.

CHAPTER III: GENERAL PROCEDURAL PROVISIONS

Rule 19: Procedural Orders

The Commission shall make the orders required for the conduct of the proceeding.

Rule 20: Preliminary Procedural Consultation

(1) As early as possible after the constitution of a Commission, its President shall endeavor to ascertain the views of the parties regarding questions of procedure. For this purpose he may request the parties to

(a) the number of members of the Commission required to constitute a quorum at its sittings;

(b) the language or languages to be used in the proceeding;

(c) the evidence, oral or written, which each party intends to produce or to request the Commission to call for, and the written statements which each party intends to file, as well as the time limits within which such evidence should be produced and such statements filed;

(d) the number of copies desired by each party of instruments filed by the other; and

(e) the manner in which the record of the hearings shall be kept.

(2) In the conduct of the proceeding the Commission shall apply any agreement between the parties on procedural matters, except as otherwise provided in the Convention or the Administrative and Financial Regulations.

Rule 21: Procedural Languages

(1) The parties may agree on the use of one or two languages to be used in the proceeding, provided that, if they agree on any language that is not an official language of the Centre, the Commission, after consultation with the Secretary-General, gives its approval. If the parties do not agree on any such procedural language, each of them may select one of the official languages (i.e., English, French and Spanish) for this purpose.

(2) If two procedural languages are selected by the parties, any instrument may be filed in either language. Either language may be used at the hearings, subject, if the Commission so requires, to translation and interpretation. The recommendations and the report of the Commission shall be rendered and the record kept in both procedural languages, both versions being equally authentic.

CHAPTER IV: CONCILIATION PROCEDURES

Rule 22: Functions of the Commission

(1) In order to clarify the issues in dispute between the parties, the Commission shall hear the parties and shall endeavor to obtain any information that might serve this end. The parties shall be associated with its work as closely as possible.

(2) In order to bring about agreement between the parties, the Commission may, from time to time at any stage of the proceeding, make—orally or in writing—recommendations to the parties. It may recommend that the parties accept specific terms of settlement or that they refrain, while it seeks to bring about agreement between them, from specific acts that might aggravate the dispute; it shall point out to the parties the arguments in favor of its recommendations. It may fix time limits within which each party shall inform the Commission of its decision concerning the recommendations made.

(3) The Commission, in order to obtain information that might enable it to discharge its functions, may at any stage of the proceeding:

(a) request from either party oral explanations, documents and other information;

(b) request evidence from other persons; and

(c) with the consent of the party concerned, visit any place connected with the dispute or conduct inquiries there, provided that the parties may participate in any such visits and inquiries.

Rule 23: Cooperation of the Parties

(1) The parties shall cooperate in good faith with the Commission and, in particular, at its request furnish all relevant documents, information and explanations as well as use the means at their disposal to enable the Commission to hear witnesses and experts whom it desires to call. The parties shall also facilitate visits to and inquiries at any place connected with the dispute that the Commission desires to undertake.

(2) The parties shall comply with any time limits agreed with or fixed by the Commission.

Rule 24: Transmission of the Request

As soon as the Commission is constituted, the Secretary-General shall transmit to each member a copy of the request by which the proceeding was initiated, of the supporting documentation, of the notice of registration and of any communication received from either party in response thereto.

Rule 25: Written Statements

(1) Upon the constitution of the Commission, its President shall invite each party to file, within 30 days or such longer time limit as he may fix, a written statement of its position. If, upon its constitution, the Commission has no

President, such invitation shall be issued and any such longer time limit shall be fixed by the Secretary-General. At any stage of the proceeding, within such time limits as the Commission shall fix, either party may file such other written statements as it deems useful and relevant.
(2) Except as otherwise provided by the Commission after consultation with the parties and the Secretary-General, every written statement or other instrument shall be filed in the form of a signed original accompanied by additional copies whose number shall be two more than the number of members of the Commission.

Rule 26: Supporting Documentation

(1) Every written statement or other instrument filed by a party may be accompanied by supporting documentation, in such form and number of copies as required by Administrative and Financial Regulation 30.
(2) Supporting documentation shall ordinarily be filed together with the instrument to which it relates, and in any case within the time limit fixed for the filing of such instrument.

Rule 27: Hearings

(1) The hearings of the Commission shall take place in private and, except as the parties otherwise agree, shall remain secret.
(2) The Commission shall decide, with the consent of the parties, which other persons besides the parties, their agents, counsel and advocates, witnesses and experts during their testimony, and officers of the Commission may attend the hearings.

Rule 28: Witnesses and Experts

(1) Each party may, at any stage of the proceeding, request that the Commission hear the witnesses and experts whose evidence the party considers relevant. The Commission shall fix a time limit within which such hearing shall take place.
(2) Witnesses and experts shall, as a rule, be examined before the Commission by the parties under the control of its President. Questions may also be put to them by any member of the Commission.
(3) If a witness or expert is unable to appear before it, the Commission, in agreement with the parties, may make appropriate arrangements for the evidence to be given in a written deposition or to be taken by examination elsewhere. The parties may participate in any such examination.

CHAPTER V: TERMINATION OF THE PROCEEDING

Rule 29: Objections to Jurisdiction

(1) Any objection that the dispute is not within the jurisdiction of the Centre or, for other reasons, is not within the competence of the Commission shall be

made as early as possible. A party shall file the objection with the Secretary-General no later than in its first written statement or at the first hearing if that occurs earlier, unless the facts on which the objection is based are unknown to the party at that time.
(2) The Commission may on its own initiative consider, at any stage of the proceeding, whether the dispute before it is within the jurisdiction of the Centre and within its own competence.
(3) Upon the formal raising of an objection, the proceeding on the merits shall be suspended. The Commission shall obtain the views of the parties on the objection.
(4) The Commission may deal with the objection as a preliminary question or join it to the merits of the dispute. If the Commission overrules the objection or joins it to the merits, it shall resume consideration of the latter without delay.
(5) If the Commission decides that the dispute is not within the jurisdiction of the Centre or not within its own competence, it shall close the proceeding and draw up a report to that effect, in which it shall state its reasons.

Rule 30: Closure of the Proceeding

(1) If the parties reach agreement on the issues in dispute, the Commission shall close the proceeding and draw up its report noting the issues in dispute and recording that the parties have reached agreement. At the request of the parties, the report shall record the detailed terms and conditions of their agreement.
(2) If at any stage of the proceeding it appears to the Commission that there is no likelihood of agreement between the parties, the Commission shall, after notice to the parties, close the proceeding and draw up its report noting the submission of the dispute to conciliation and recording the failure of the parties to reach agreement.
(3) If one party fails to appear or participate in the proceeding, the Commission shall, after notice to the parties, close the proceeding and draw up its report noting the submission of the dispute to conciliation and recording the failure of that party to appear or participate.

Rule 31: Preparation of the Report

The report of the Commission shall be drawn up and signed within 60 days after the closure of the proceeding.

Rule 32: The Report

(1) The report shall be in writing and shall contain, in addition to the material specified in paragraph (2) and in Rule 30:
- (a) a precise designation of each party;
- (b) a statement that the Commission was established under the Convention, and a description of the method of its constitution;

(c) the names of the members of the Commission, and an identification of the appointing authority of each;
(d) the names of the agents, counsel and advocates of the parties;
(e) the dates and place of the sittings of the Commission; and
(f) a summary of the proceeding.

(2) The report shall also record any agreement of the parties, pursuant to Article 35 of the Convention, concerning the use in other proceedings of the views expressed or statements or admissions or offers of settlement made in the proceeding before the Commission or of the report or any recommendation made by the Commission.

(3) The report shall be signed by the members of the Commission; the date of each signature shall be indicated. The fact that a member refuses to sign the report shall be recorded therein.

Rule 33: Communication of the Report

(1) Upon signature by the last conciliator to sign, the Secretary-General shall promptly:

(a) authenticate the original text of the report and deposit it in the archives of the Centre; and
(b) dispatch a certified copy to each party, indicating the date of dispatch on the original text and on all copies.

(2) The Secretary-General shall, upon request, make available to a party additional certified copies of the report.

(3) The Centre shall not publish the report without the consent of the parties.

CHAPTER VI: GENERAL PROVISIONS

Rule 34: Final Provisions

(1) The texts of these Rules in each official language of the Centre shall be equally authentic.

(2) These Rules may be cited as the "Conciliation Rules" of the Centre.

PRIMARY SOURCES

Alternative Dispute Resolution. A Report Prepared by Henry Brown for the Courts and Legal Services Committee, *The Law Society*, Legal Practice Directorate, July 1991

CEDR Model ADR Contract Clauses adopted in September 1999

CEDR Model Mediation Procedure and Agreement adopted in February 1999

Heilbron Report, 1993, HMSO, Lord Chancellor's Department

General Treaty of Friendship, Commerce and Navigation, 1794, between the United Kingdom and the United States; see further J Simpson and H Fox, *International Arbitration: Law and Practice*, Stevens & Sons, London (1959)

Guide to Arbitration published by CAS, Lausanne

ICC Arbitration Rules

Halsbury's Law of England, 4th Edition

Mediation Rules of the International Council of Arbitration for Sports (ICAS)

Practice Direction issued by the Family Division of the High Court on 2 November 1982, published in [1982] 1 WLR at 1420

Practice Direction (Family Division: Conciliation Procedure) (No. 2) published in [1984] WLR 1326

Practice Direction *"Ancillary Relief Procedure – Pilot Scheme"* dated 16 June 1997 published in [1977] 3 ALL ER 768

Practice Direction dated 25 May 2000 Reproduced in [2000] 3 ALL ER 379

Practice Note published in [1994] 1 ALL ER 34

Practice Note published in [1995] 1 ALL ER 385

Pre-application Protocol

Report of the Committee on Alternative Dispute Resolution, General Council of the Bar, October 1991

Mediation Rules of the Stockholm Chamber of Commerce Mediation Institute (1 April 1999)

Rules for the Policy adopted by ICANN on 24 October 1991

Rules of the London Court of International Arbitration

Society of Professionals in Dispute Resolution ("SPDR"), the United States, (1990) Draft Report entitled *Mandatory Participation and Settlement Coercion; Dispute Resolution as it Relates to the Courts.*

Supplemental Rules for the Policy of the WIPO Arbitration and Mediation Center

The Woolf Report – *Access to Justice* by The Right Honourable the Lord Woolf

UNCITRAL Arbitration Rules

Uniform Domain Name Dispute Resolution Policy adopted by the Internet Corporation for Assigned Names and Numbers (ICANN) on 26 August 1999

WIPO Mediation Rules, Article 1 at http://www.wipo.int/amc/en/mediation/rules/index.html

OTHER SOURCES

Abel, R L (ed)	*The Politics of Informal Justice Justice, Volume 1: The American Experience*, Academic Press, New York and London (1982)
Ackland, A F	*A Sudden Break of Commons Sense: Managing Conflict through Mediation*, London, Hutchinson Business Books (1990)
Adler, Hensler & Nelson	*Simple Justice: How Litigants Fare in the Pittsburgh Court Arbitration Program* (1983) 629-637
Auerbach, J S	*Justice Without Law? Resolving Disputes Without Lawyers* (1984), Oxford University Press, Oxford
Bingham, Gail	*Resolving Environmental Disputes: A Decade of Experience*, The Conservation Foundation (1986)
Brown, H and Marriott, A	*ADR: Principles and Practice*, London, Sweet & Maxwell (1993)
Bush, R A B	*Efficiency and Protection, or Empowerment and Recognition?: The Mediator's Role and Ethical Standards in Mediation, 41 Florida Law Review* (1989) 253
Caroll, E and Mackie, K J	*International Mediation: The Art of Business Diplomacy,* Kluwer International (1999)
CEDR	*Court Referred ADR – A Guide for the Judiciary*, CEDR, (1999)
Chatterjee, C	*Negotiating Techniques in International Contracts*, Aldershot, Ashgate (2000)
—	"Investment-related Promissory Notes are Investments under the ICSID Convention: *Fedax NV v The Republic of Venezuela*", 3 *The Journal of World Investment* (2002) 147
Chatterjee, S K	"Whether the Award of a Rent Review Tribunal is Admissible in Arbitration, 61 *Arbitration* (1995) 293
—	"Do Disputes arise 'out of' or 'under' or 'out of and under' a Contract?", *Arbitration* (1994) 117–122
Colosi, T	"Negotiations in the Public and Private Sectors" (1983) 27(2), *American Behavioral Scientist* 229
Cot, Jean-Pierre	*International Conciliation*, London, Europa Publications (1968)

Cross, R and Tapper, C	*Cross and Tapper on Evidence*, LexisNexis UK (2003)
Davis, Gwynn	"Mediation Appointments on Money and Property in the Bristol County Court", *Family Law* (April 1991)
Fisher, R and Ury, W	*Getting to Yes,* Boston, Massachusetts: Houghton Mifflin (1981)
Fiss, O M	"Against Settlement" 93 *Yale Law Journal* (1984) 1073
Goffman, E	*The Presentation of Self in Everyday Life*, New York, Anchor Books (1959)
Gulliver, P	*Disputes and Negotiations: A Cross-Cultural Perspective*, Academic Press, New York and London (1979)
Harter, Philip J	"Negotiating Regulations: A Cure for Malaise", 71 *Georgetown L.J.* (1982)
Hensler, D	"Court-Annexed ADR," in Wilkinson, J. H. (ed.), *Donovan Leisure Newton & Irvine ADR Practice Book*, New York, John Wiley & Sons (1990)
Kessler, G and Finkelstein, L J	"The Evolution of a Multi-door Courthouse", 37 *Cath. U.L. Rev.* (1988) 577
Lauterpacht, H	*The Development of International Law by the International Court*, London, Stevens (1958)
Levine, D I	"Early Neutral Evaluation: A Follow-up Report", *Judicature*, vol 70 (1987)
	"Early Neutral Evaluation: The Second Phase", *Journal of Dispute Resolution*, Vol 1989 at 1
Mackie, K J and Carroll, E	*ADR Route Map*, CEDR (1998)
Mackie, K J, Marsh, W and Miles, D	*Commercial Dispute Resolution – An ADR Practice Guide*, London, Butterworth (1995)
McThenia, A W and Shaffer, T L	"For Reconciliation", 94 *Yale Law Journal* (1985) 1660
Moore, Christopher W	*The Mediation Process: Practical Strategies for Resolving Conflict*, San Francisco, Jossey-Bass (1986)
Murray, J S, Rau, A S and Sherman, E F	*Processes of Dispute Resolution: The Role of Lawyers*, Westbury, New York, Foundation Press (1989)
Noone, M	*Mediation,* London, Cavendish Press (1996)

Odams, A M and Higgins, J	*Commercial Dispute Resolution*, London, Construction Law Press (1996)
Palmer, M	"The Revival of Mediation in the People's Republic of China: (1) Extra-judicial mediation", in Butler, W E (ed) *Yearbook on Socialist Legal Systems* (1987)
Palmer, M and Simon, R	*Dispute Process: ADR and the Primary Forms of Decision Making*, London, Butterworth (1998)
Parker, D and Parkinson, A	"Solicitors and Family Conciliation Service: A Basis for Professional Co-operation", 15 *Family Law* (1985) 270
Roberts, S	*Mediation and Family Disputes, Modern Law Review*, 1983 at 555
Roscoe, P	"The Causes of Popular Dissatisfaction with the Administration of Justice", *American Bar Association Report*, Vol. 29, Part 1, (1906) pp 395–417
Rose, G and Girlis, S (District Judges)	"Conciliation for Family Finance", *Family Law* (March 1991)
Rubino-Sammartano, M	*International Arbitration Law*, The Hague, Kluwer (1990)
Simmel, G	*The Sociology of Georg Simmel,* edited by K Wolff, Glencoe, Illinois, Free Press (1950, originally 1908)
Simpson, J L and Fox, H	*International Arbitration*, London, Sweet & Maxwell
Susskind, L and Cruikshank, J	*Breaking the Impasse: Consensual Approaches to Resolving Public Disputes*, New York, Basic Books (1987)

Index